How We Got Our Bible

How We Got Our Bible

RALPH EARLE

Revised and edited by David J. Felter and Jim Edlin

BEACON HILL PRESS

OF KANSAS CITY

First edition 1971
Second edition 1992
Third edition 2010

ISBN 978-0-8341-2495-0

Printed in the
United States of America

Cover design: Brandon Hill
Interior design: Sharon Page
Photo credits:
 pp. 19, 37, 66, 67, 68, 70, 71, 75, 87, 94, 101—© 2010 Jupiterimages Corporation
 p. 50—Snark/Art Resource, NY
 pp. 58, 65—HIP/Art Resource, NY
 p. 77—Nazarene Publishing House

Library of Congress Cataloging-in-Publication Data

Earle, Ralph.
  How we got our Bible / Ralph Earle ; revised and edited by David J. Felter and Jim Edlin. — 3rd ed.
    p. cm.
  Includes bibliographical references.
  ISBN 978-0-8341-2495-0 (pbk.)
  1. Bible—History. 2. Bible—Versions. I. Felter, David J. II. Edlin, Jim, 1950-
III. Title.
  BS445.E2 2010
  220.1'2—dc22

                                                    2010000677

10 9 8 7 6 5 4 3 2 1

Contents

Preface to the First Edition

One of the most heartening trends of the last several years has been the increased interest in the study of the Bible. As far as we can discover, in the first fifty years of this century (1900-1949) there appeared only about half a dozen significant new series of English commentaries on the Bible (or New Testament). In the next ten years (1950-59) no fewer than ten were begun. Here is a partial list:

1. "Bible Commentary" (Lutheran)
2. "Cambridge Greek Testament Commentary"
3. "Daily Study Bible" (William Barclay)
4. "Epworth Preacher's Commentaries"
5. "Evangelical Commentary on the Bible"
6. "Harper's New Testament Commentaries"
7. *Laymen's Bible Commentary*
8. "New International Commentary"
9. *New Testament Commentary* (William Hendriksen)
10. "Tyndale New Testament Commentaries"

During the next decade (1960-69) several other new series were started. These include

1. "The Anchor Bible"
2. *Beacon Bible Commentary*
3. "Cambridge Bible Commentary"
4. "New Clarendon Bible"
5. *Wesleyan Bible Commentary*

Some of these series (quotation marks) or sets (italics) run into many volumes. For instance, "The Anchor Bible"—the first such joint project of Catholics, Protestants, and Jews—is scheduled for fifty volumes.

In addition, there are many smaller books on Bible study, most of them written by Evangelicals. Add to this the large crop of new translations of the Bible, and it is easy to see the Book of Books is being read and studied by many people. We give God thanks for this continuing interest in His Word.

A basic question for all of us is—How did we get our Bible? This book, in a brief survey of the subject, seeks to answer that question.

—Ralph Earle

Preface to the Third Edition

Since Ralph Earle wrote his Preface in 1971, interest in the Bible has only continued to increase. Each year a multitude of user-friendly resources for Bible study are regularly published. This present text intends to make an important contribution to this collection by providing a very readable and informative overview of the origins of the Bible.

Working on the revision of this book has been a great privilege for me. As a student in Ralph Earle's classes at Nazarene Theological Seminary in Kansas City, I never dreamed of an opportunity to become involved in one of his writing projects. I sat in awe of his encyclopedic mind and also of his character. His leading role on the NIV translation committee at the time made his classes fascinating.

Dr. Earle was a world-class scholar, a captivating teacher, and a passionate preacher. He humbly embodied the Holiness message he so unashamedly proclaimed around the world in churches and camp meetings. He was truly a gentleman's gentleman as well as a scholar's scholar.

It is because of Ralph Earle's vibrant spirit that I am so excited to assist in this revision. I am hopeful that another generation will be able to experience his unbounded enthusiasm for God's Word and extensive knowledge of it. The text still remains largely his. I have updated some materials on the basis of more recent scholarship and added information about translations that emerged since his writing and David Felter's revision. At times I endeavored to make the text more readable for a twenty-first-century audience, although in many ways Ralph Earle's style is timeless.

I am sure Dr. Earle's prayer would be the same as mine—may this book be the means to kindle a compelling love for God's Word among all those who read it.

—Jim Edlin

Prologue

A lonely shepherd sat on the backside of the desert. All was still—no blaring radio, glaring television, ringing doorbell or telephone; no rumble of distant traffic or roar of jets piercing the sky. Not a sound shattered the silence; not a sight of moving humanity or beast greeted his eye.

A later psalmist wrote, "Be still, and know that I am God" (Psalm 46:10). In the stillness of that distant day a grateful shepherd met the Great Shepherd. From leading a few sheep of his father-in-law, he was called to lead the large flock of God's people.

The solitude gave wings to his thoughts. He remembered the stories his devout mother told him—of Adam and Eve, of Cain and Abel, of Noah and the Flood, of Abraham, Isaac, Jacob, and Joseph. Little did he realize that under the inspiration of the divine Holy Spirit he would one day be the human instrument for preserving these stories for generations to come.

His mind went back over his own lifetime. A cruel Pharaoh had given orders to kill all the male children of Israel. As a baby, Moses was miraculously preserved from death. Adopted by Pharaoh's daughter, he was brought up in the royal palace. He was carefully educated "in all the wisdom of the Egyptians and was powerful in speech and action" (Acts 7:22). Egypt was the greatest empire of that day. It was the leading center of learning. God was preparing His servant for a twofold task. His training prepared him to be the founder of the nation of Israel. His schooling in the great literature of that day was priceless. It prepared him to become the first scribe of divine Scripture.

At the age of forty, Moses made an important decision. He left the court of Pharaoh and joined the struggles of his own persecuted people. By God's help, he would deliver them from oppression and slavery.

Moses' first mistake was attempting this in his own strength and wisdom. Watching a Hebrew slave being beaten, Moses killed the attacker. Pharaoh heard about it, and Moses had to run for his life.

Forty years passed. During this frustrating time, Moses learned valuable lessons of patience. Something else happened. Far removed from palace life in Egypt, he discovered an awareness of God's presence. Meditation and study became his most important vocation. He learned much that was not in the wisdom books of Egypt.

While watching his flock one day he noticed a bush burning nearby. Had the blazing sun ignited it? Why was the bush not consumed in the flames? Curious, Moses stepped nearer for a better look. Out of the burning bush came the voice of God. The great "I Am" revealed himself as the God of Abraham, Isaac, and Jacob, and the Redeemer of Israel. Here Moses received his call to be the messenger of God. He was to deliver the Israelites from Egyptian bondage and give them the divine law. Moses would record the story of creation and God's dealings with humanity. He was to write the first chapters of salvation history, the beginnings of our Bible.

One
Its
Origin

There are two definitive passages in the New Testament on the subject of inspiration. One is 2 Timothy 3:16: "All scripture is inspired by God and is useful for teaching, for reproof, for correction, and for training in righteousness" (NRSV). The phrase "inspired by God" is all one word in Greek, *theopneustos*—literally, God-breathed, as the NIV has it. Sacred Scripture was breathed out by God and into human minds by the Holy Spirit. Thus, the Bible is "the 'Spirit-breathed' expression of God's Word" to us.[1] Clement of Alexandria (second century) and Origen (third century) use this term to describe the Scriptures.

The second passage is 2 Peter 1:21—"Prophecy never had its origin in the will of man, but men spoke from God as they were carried along by the Holy Spirit." Literally the second half of this verse reads, "But being borne along by the Holy Spirit, men spoke from God." The Holy Spirit lifted human writers of the Bible to a higher level of spiritual understanding. From this level they could receive divine truth and communicate it to believers.

On the basis of these two passages and others, we can clearly see with H. Ray Dunning that "the idea of the 'inspiredness' of Scripture is a biblical truth."[2]

James Arminius was a Dutch theologian who was born in 1560 and died in 1609. Regarding the Bible, he wrote, "We now have the infallible word of God in no other place than in the Scriptures."[3]

He goes on to make this helpful statement:

The primary cause of these books is God, in his Son, through the Holy Spirit. The instrumental causes are holy men of God, who, not at their own will and pleasure, but as they were actuated and inspired by the Holy Spirit wrote these books, whether the words were inspired into them, dictated to them, or administered by them under divine direction.[4]

This passage suggests three degrees of inspiration for different parts of the Bible. First there is eternal truth—which could not otherwise be known by the human intellect—"inspired into"; that is, breathed out of God and into the hearts and minds of the writers. In the second place, some parts of the Scripture seem actually to have been dictated, as in the case of the law given to Moses at Sinai. But other parts of the Bible were simply "administered to them under divine direction." These would include the genealogical tables, as in the first nine chapters of 1 Chronicles, and other historical documents that the authors were led by the Spirit to incorporate into their writings.

It was John Wesley in the eighteenth century who took the theology of James Arminius, making it a powerful force, bringing the great spiritual revival to England. In the preface to his *Explanatory Notes upon the New Testament* he says of sacred Scripture, "Every part thereof is worthy of God; and all together are one entire body, wherein is no defect, no excess."[5]

In the same connection he writes, "The language of His messengers, also, is exact in the highest degree: for the words which were given them accurately answered to the impressions made upon their minds."[6]

Commenting on 2 Timothy 3:16, Wesley writes, "The Spirit of God not only once inspired those who wrote it [the Scriptures] but continually inspires, supernaturally assists, those who read it with earnest prayer."[7] Frank Moore, a contemporary Wesleyan theologian, expands on this thought when he writes, "The Bible lives because the Holy Spirit of God empowers it with His presence. We read words on a page, but we hear the voice of God speaking to our hearts through His Spirit."[8]

An important Wesleyan theologian of the past, W. B. Pope, in his three-volume *Compendium of Christian Theology* (first published in 1875-76), devotes thirty-seven pages to the subject of the inspiration of the Bible. He writes of the Bible—

Its plenary inspiration makes Holy Scripture the absolute and final authority, all-sufficient as the Supreme Standard of Faith, Directory of Morals, and Charter of Privileges to the Church of God. Of course, the Book of Divine revelations cannot contain anything untrue; but its infallibility is by itself especially connected with religious truth. . . . It is after all, a Divine-human collection of documents: the precise relation of the human to the Divine is a problem which has engaged much attention, and has not yet been, though it may yet be, adequately solved. But in the domain of religious truth, and the kingdom of God among men, its claim to authority and sufficiency is absolute.[9]

Nazarenes regard H. Orton Wiley as the outstanding Arminian theologian of the twentieth century. His definition of inspiration follows: "By Inspiration we mean the actuating energy of the Holy Spirit by which holy men were qualified to receive religious truth and to communicate it to others without error."[10]

Wiley believed the Bible was fully inspired. He says the Scriptures were "given by plenary inspiration, embracing throughout the elements of superintendence, elevation and suggestion, in that manner and to that degree that the Bible becomes the infallible word of God, the authoritative Rule of Faith and Practice in the Church."[11]

A contemporary Wesleyan theologian, J. Kenneth Grider, articulates this perspective as follows: "Wesleyan-Holiness Evangelicals understand that God inspired prophets and apostles and others with thoughts that they were to write down, but He left to them, in their intelligent and redeemed freedom, the choices of words with which to write down the inspired thoughts."[12]

A Divine-Human Book

The Bible is a divine-human Book, as Christ is the divine-human Person. This is the key that unlocks the door to understanding the true nature of the Scriptures.

God could have sent His Son in adult human form without a human birth. Jesus' body would then have been simply a shell in which the divine nature was encased.

God in His wisdom did not choose to do it this way. He caused His Son to be born of a woman. Jesus shared the personality characteristics of His mother—psychologically as well as physically. He not only bore physical resemblance to her but also was influenced by all the environmental factors of His home. He was the son of Mary as well as the Son of God.

So it is with the Bible. God could have sent down the Book all inscribed with the complete revelation. He could have bound it in black leather, with gold edges, silk-sewn on India paper. But He did not choose to do so. Instead, the light of divine revelation broke in on the soul of Moses, David, Paul, John, and many others. The result is a divinely inspired, humanly written revelation of God's truth for humanity.

Scripture writers wrote on sheepskin, goatskin, papyrus, and parchment. They wrote the thoughts of God as they understood them with the help of the Holy Spirit.

As sunlight is conducted through a prism and is broken into various rays, so the light of God's truth, filtered through prisms of human personality, takes on varying slants and interests. This appears in the language used—both vocabulary and style—and in the thought forms they use. Different approaches and diversity of emphasis also appear. The Holy Spirit uses these varying interests and emphases to bring the total of divine revelation in the Bible.

It is unfortunate that too often we see only one side of truth, and so we actually have only a half-truth. Ask Evangelicals, "Was Jesus divine or human?" They will answer emphatically, "Divine!" Ask humanists the same question, and the reply will be "Human." Both are right, and both are wrong. The opposition between Jesus' deity and humanity exists only in false theological thinking. Jesus was, and is, both human and divine.

The same situation occurs when Evangelicals emphasize the divine source of the Bible at the neglect of its human origin. Liberals stress the latter and forget the former. The Bible did have a human origin; it came from the hands of the men who wrote it. Its ultimate source, however, was divine. The Holy Spirit inspired the writers. It is this inspiration that gives it its unique authority as the Word of God.

One man sees only the scribe sitting at a desk, pen in hand, writing the words of scripture, and he declares, "The Bible is a human book." Another sees only the inspiring Spirit hovering overhead, and he cries, "It is divine!" What we need is to see the whole picture, not just one part of it. The Bible is a divine-human book.

In the Preface to his sermons John Wesley wrote these beautiful words:

> I have thought, I am a creature of a day, passing through life as an arrow through the air. I am a spirit come from God, and returning to God: Just hovering over the great gulf; till a few moments hence, I am no more seen; I drop into an unchangeable eternity! I want to know one thing—the way to heaven; how to land safe on that happy shore. God himself has condescended to teach the way: For this very end he came from heaven. He hath written it down in a book. O give me that book! At any price, give me the book of God! I have it: Here is knowledge enough for me. Let me be *homo unius libri* [a man of one Book].[13]

The Pages Appear

Morning dawned over the camp of Israel. Suddenly the silence of the disappearing night was shattered. Rumbling thunder roared overhead.

Nervously the people pulled aside their tent flaps and looked out just in time to see another blinding light streak across the sky. Now the lightning was flashing and the thunder crashing. Out of the thick cloud that covered the top of Mount Sinai a trumpet blast came, loud and long. All the people stood in their tent openings, trembling with fear.

As they looked up at the sacred mountain, smoke billowed from its peak as if from a giant smokestack, "because the LORD descended on it in fire" (Exodus 19:18). It seemed now the hill was one big, smoldering furnace. To add to the people's terror, the whole mountain shook with a violent earthquake.

One man was unafraid. He had met God at the burning bush, right in this same place (3:2). So he called out, and God answered him (19:19). Moses was called to the top of Mount Sinai. That day the Ten Commandments were given (chapter 20). Israel was to be the people of the covenant, the people of the Book. Moses was God's scribe, to give them the Book of the Law.

Traditionally the first five books of our Bible are assigned to Moses. For the material recorded in Genesis, Moses would have had to depend on oral traditions, handed down from generation to generation and on the direct inspiration of the Holy Spirit. As far as the Genesis record of the creation of the world and of human life is concerned, this would all have had to be given by divine revelation, for no person was present to see these events and tell about them.

When it came to the materials of Exodus, Leviticus, Numbers, and Deuteronomy, Moses was the man most involved. No one could have written this down better than he.

It should be noted, however, that Moses obviously did not write the last chapter of Deuteronomy. Here we find an account of Moses' death and burial, with the added statement "But to this day no one knows where his grave is" (34:6). A further observation is made: "Since then, no prophet has risen in Israel like Moses, whom the LORD knew face to face" (verse 10). To say Moses himself wrote these words beforehand by divine inspiration—as some have claimed—is unrealistic. The whole tenor of the terminology used here clearly points to a later generation, when the monumental work of Moses was edited in its final form.

The Books Multiply

Joshua was Moses' successor, and the sixth book of our Old Testament is named for him. It records his great achievements in leading the Israelites across the Jordan River. They conquered the land of Canaan, and each tribe was assigned its territory. The book naturally divides at the middle into two parts. The first (chapters 1–12) tells of the conquest of Canaan. The second (chapters 13–24) records the partition of the land.

The fact that Joshua's name is attached to the book does not mean he wrote it. In the last chapter we find the record of the death and burial of God's great warrior (24:29-30). Then comes the statement "Israel served the LORD throughout the lifetime of Joshua and of the elders who outlived him and who had experienced everything the LORD had done for Israel" (verse 31). It is clear, at least in its finished form, the Book of Joshua was written in a later generation. We do not know who wrote it.

The same is said of the Book of Judges, which fills in the time from Joshua to Samuel. The keynote of this book is—"In those days Israel had no king; everyone did as he saw fit" (17:6; 21:25). With no central government, the Israelites too often lived in chaotic confusion. The recurring sequence in Judges is disobedience, oppression, repentance, and deliverance. The so-called judges were for the most part sent by God to deliver the people from their oppressors.

The little love story called **Ruth** gives a brief picture of life in that period (1:1). Its purpose may have been to fill in one point in the ancestry of King David (4:17-22).

The two books of **Samuel** cover the period of the great prophet by the same name. They also cover the reigns of Saul and David, the first two kings of Israel—both of whom were anointed by Samuel. The narrative begins with the birth of this man (1 Samuel 1) and his call to the prophetic ministry (chapter 3). Samuel devoted a long lifetime to ruling Israel as a judge. Unfortunately, he failed to train his own children to follow in his footsteps (8:1-5). And so the people asked for a king. In answer to their plea, God instructed Samuel to anoint Saul as the first king over Israel. Saul became stubborn and disobedient, and his life ended in disaster. His successor was David, the importance of whose reign is shown by the fact the entire book of 2 Samuel is devoted to it.

The two books of **Kings** describe the reign of Solomon over the United Kingdom of Israel—which had been carved out by his father, David. They also cover the period of the divided monarchy. The Northern Kingdom of Israel was ruled by several dynasties, beginning with Jeroboam. It came to an end in 722/21 B.C. with the capture of its capital city, Samaria, by the Assyrians, and the deportation of the people to Mesopotamia (2 Kings 17:6). To fill the vacancy, the king of Assyria brought people from the East and settled them in the cities of Samaria (verse 24). The result was a group known as the Samaritans of Jesus' day.

An interesting feature of the history of northern Israel is the appearance of the two prophets, Elijah and Elisha. They sought to call the idolatrous Israelites back to the worship of the true God but with limited results.

The Southern Kingdom of Judah was ruled by the dynasty of David. It came to an end in 586/87 B.C. with the fall of Jerusalem to the Babylonians. Except for the eighty years of Maccabean independence (142 to 63), there was no independent nation of Israel from 586/87 B.C. to A.D. 1948, when the new state of Israel was set up.

The observant reader may have noted two things in our discussion so far. First we have given no dates prior to 1000 B.C. This is for the simple reason that archaeologists are not in universal agreement about the chronology of events before the time of David. The second feature is the use of double dating, such as 722/21 B.C. This is because events in ancient time are usually dated in a certain year of some king's reign. So often we cannot be sure within a year as to the exact date.

Who wrote the books of Samuel and Kings cannot be determined. The fact that they bring the history of Israel down to the time of the exile suggests their composition came at that time. However, this does not mean the stories in them were written down only then. These books were likely the product of a growing collection of materials that came together over several centuries of the Israelite monarchy.

The two books of **Chronicles** cover a much wider period than the books of Kings. In fact, the genealogical tables in the first nine chapters go back to Adam (1 Chronicles 1:1). The historical narrative begins with the death of Saul (chapter 10). The rest of 1 Chronicles is taken up with the reign of David. Second Chronicles describes the rule of Solomon and carries us down through the period of the divided kingdom. The last two verses

(2 Chronicles 36:22-23) give the decree of Cyrus (538 B.C.) for the return of the captives to Judah. It is obvious the Chronicles were not written until after the Babylonian captivity. They reflect in their opening chapters the greatly increased interest in genealogies characteristic of the postexilic period. To be accepted, the returning captives had to prove their Jewish ancestry. The same feature is prominent in the two following books, Ezra and Nehemiah.

Ezra begins at the point where 2 Chronicles ends—with the decree of Cyrus (Ezra 1:1-4), which was followed soon (536 B.C.) by the first return from Babylonian captivity under Zerubbabel (chapter 2). Ezra's main interest described here is the rebuilding of the Temple (chapters 3–6). Another group returned (458 B.C.) under Ezra himself (chapters 7–8). His primary concern was to restore the true worship of God (chapters 9–10).

The Book of **Nehemiah** is written in the first person, as are parts of **Ezra** (chapters 8–9). Nehemiah went to Jerusalem (around 444 B.C.) for the express purpose of rebuilding its walls, which still lay in ruins.

The personalities of these two men are a study in contrasts. When Ezra heard some of the returned captives were disobeying the Lord's commands, "I tore my tunic and cloak, pulled hair from my head and beard and sat down appalled" (Ezra 9:3). When Nehemiah met the same situation, he says, "I beat some of the men and pulled out their hair" (Nehemiah 13:25). Of course, Nehemiah was the king's appointed governor, while Ezra was a priest and scribe. God could use both of these very different men to do an important work in His kingdom.

The Book of **Esther** belongs to the Persian (postexilic) period, in company with Ezra and Nehemiah. Its purpose is perhaps to explain the origin of the Jewish Feast of Purim (Esther 9:26).

According to 9:20, Mordecai may be responsible for at least the first edition of this book.

There is no way of knowing just when the Book of **Job** was written. Its setting is "in the land of Uz" (1:1), which probably means the great Syrian desert east and northeast of Palestine. It deals with the timeless, universal problem of human suffering. In literary form it is a majestic drama, discussing the lofty subject of God's dealings with people. As in the case of all devotional classics, its time of writing is unimportant. Along with the Proverbs and Ecclesiastes, it belongs to the "Wisdom Literature" of the Old Testament. It shares striking resemblances in some points with the wisdom literature of ancient Egypt and Babylonia.

The **Psalms** were a hymnal for the Israelites. About half the one hundred fifty psalms are attributed to David. Most of the others are anonymous. Their dates probably stretch from the time of David to the Exile.

The Book of **Proverbs** is stated (1:1; 10:1) as consisting largely of wise sayings written or collected by Solomon. Some two hundred years later, the scribes of Hezekiah reportedly copied chapters 25-29 (25:1). The last two chapters are attributed respectively to Agur and King Lemuel. It is obvious that Proverbs is a collection of wisdom sayings, gathered over a considerable period of time.

Ecclesiastes (or "The Preacher") is credited to the "son of David, king in Jerusalem" (1:1). Its main theme is sounded at once: "'Meaningless! Meaningless!' says the Teacher. 'Utterly meaningless! Everything is meaningless'" (verse 2). Such is all life lived "under the sun" (verse 3), without reference to God above. "Meaningless" or "vanity" (KJV and NRSV) literally means emptiness.

The **Song of Songs** is sometimes called Canticles. It is also attributed to King Solomon (1:1). In typical Oriental language it describes the joys of marital love. There is a difference of opinion among commentators as to whether this is to be taken as an allegory of the relationship between Christ and His Bride.

The rest of the Old Testament consists of books of prophecy. The ministry of **Isaiah** is dated from about 740 to 700 B.C. He prophesied in the Southern Kingdom of Judah and presumably wrote near the close of this period. It should be noted that many scholars argue a second Isaiah wrote chapters 40–66 during the Babylonian captivity. There is no manuscript evidence for this division. The Dead Sea Scroll of Isaiah, discovered in 1947 and dated at about 125 B.C., has the whole book as a unit.

Contemporary with Isaiah was **Hosea** (750 to 736 B.C.), who prophesied in the Northern Kingdom of Israel. He made a dramatic plea to the Lord's wayward wife, Israel, to return to her rightful husband, leaving the false gods. But it was in vain.

Amos may be the earliest of the writing prophets. He is perhaps to be dated around 760 B.C. His emphasis is on social righteousness. He preached in the northern Israel, especially at Bethel (only twelve miles north of Jerusalem).

The dates for the ministry of **Micah** are the same as those for Isaiah (740 to 700 B.C.). He, too, prophesied in the Southern Kingdom of Judah. In common with Amos, he struck out vigorously against the oppression of the poor.

These are the four prophets of the greatest prophetic age, the eighth century B.C. Some also include Joel, Obadiah, and Jonah in this period.

Joel (dated in either the eighth or fourth century) vividly describes a terrifying plague of locusts. Then he makes a twofold application: to the coming punishment of Judah and to "the day of the Lord." The latter expression is the key phrase of this book.

Obadiah may also belong to the eighth century, though many date him in the sixth century. This little book of a single chapter has one theme: the destruction of Edom, to be followed by the restoration of Israel.

According to 2 Kings 14:25, the prophet **Jonah** ministered during the reign of Jeroboam II of Israel (787 to 747 B.C.). Told to warn Nineveh of its impending doom, he tried to run away. When Nineveh repented, he complained. The book shows the folly of racial pride and also communicates God's love for all humanity.

Four prophets ministered during the seventh century: Nahum, Habakkuk, Zephaniah, and Jeremiah. **Nahum** is generally dated between 663 and 612 B.C. He predicted the destruction of Nineveh, which took place in the latter year. Israel's ancient foe, Assyria, was finally punished for its sins when the capital city fell.

Habakkuk prophesied in the same seventh century B.C., near its end (603 B.C.). He foretold the coming punishment of Judah by the Babylonians. The third chapter of his book is a prayer poem, much like those found in the Book of Psalms.

Zephaniah (about 625 B.C.) blasted out against idolatry in Judah. He pronounced judgment on Judah and foreign nations but held out hope for the salvation of a remnant.

Jeremiah prophesied during the last 40 years of the Southern Kingdom of Judah (626 to 587/86 B.C.). It was his sad task to warn the nation of its impending doom, only to see the warning go unheeded. He is called "the weeping prophet" (see 9:1). The Book of **Lamentations,** a lament over the destruction of Jerusalem, is attributed to him.

Ezekiel was the Lord's prophet to the Jewish people in Babylonian captivity. Taken in an early deportation, he apparently ministered twenty-two years (593 to 571 B.C.). In common with Isaiah and Jeremiah, Ezekiel prophesied not only to the Judeans but also to foreign nations. (These are the three longest prophetic books.) He also described a future ideal state of Israel.

As in the case of Ezekiel, **Daniel** prophesied in Babylonia (606 to 536 B.C.). The first six chapters give the history of Daniel, with visions seen by others. The last six chapters describe the visions Daniel saw. The Book of Daniel is the apocalypse of the Old Testament, though there are apocalyptic elements in other books (for example, Ezekiel).

Haggai and **Zechariah** both began their ministry at the same time (520 B.C.). The former delivered four messages in that year, all with the same theme: rebuild the Temple. Zechariah was also interested in this, as we know from Ezra 6:14. His prophecies extend from 520 to 518 B.C. A notable feature of his book is the eight visions he saw (1:7–6:15). Like most of the other prophets, he emphasized righteousness rather than ritualism.

Malachi (around 450 B.C.) is the last book of the Old Testament. The name means "my messenger." Looking across the four centuries ahead, he predicted the coming of the Messiah (3:1).

Some prophets undoubtedly wrote down their own words, while others used scribes (Jeremiah 36:4). It seems likely that, in some cases, disciples of the prophets put the books into their final forms. This could occur either during or after the lifetime of the prophet.

The New Testament Is Written

a. Paul's Letters. On their first missionary journey Paul and Barnabas founded several churches in the Roman province of Galatia (in modern Turkey). Later Paul heard of Judaizers confusing his new Gentile converts by telling them they had to be circumcised and keep the Law of Moses to be saved. Greatly disturbed, the apostle wrote a strong letter to these churches, warning them against falling from the grace of Christ into the pit of legalistic Judaism. If **Galatians** was written about the time of the Council of Jerusalem (A.D. 48), described in the fifteenth chapter of Acts, it is probably the first book of the New Testament to be written. Many scholars would date it a few years later.

On his second missionary journey Paul established a good church in Thessalonica. When he arrived at Corinth, he wrote 1 **Thessalonians,** with its twin emphases on sanctification and the Second Coming. This was in A.D. 50. It has been commonly held that this was the first book of the New Testament. 2 **Thessalonians** was written just a few months later (A.D. 51), dealing with further problems these people had about the Second Coming.

On his third missionary journey Paul spent three years at Ephesus. While there he wrote 1 **Corinthians** (A.D. 54 or 55). In it he deals with three problems occurring in the church at Corinth (chapters 1–6) and six other problems about which they had written him (chapters 7–16). These were all practical concerns with crucial implications.

After he left Ephesus, Paul wrote 2 **Corinthians** in Macedonia, probably at Philippi (A.D. 55). He was forced to defend both his ministry and his personal integrity in the face of cruel criticism from opponents in Corinth. It was the Corinthian church that gave Paul the most headaches and heartache.

It is interesting to note these first books of the New Testament are not compendiums of systematic theology. They are missionary letters, written by a missionary to churches founded on missionary journeys. They are "living letters," dealing with life among the people of God.

Sometime after his letter arrived, the busy apostle took time to visit Corinth for three months (Acts 20:3). He wanted to go on west to Rome but was collecting an offering from the Gentile churches for the poor Jewish Christians at Jerusalem. He felt he must return to the mother church there, to make sure this offering was received in a good spirit. Paul's main concern at this point was to weld the Jewish and Gentile churches into one Church of Jesus Christ.

In lieu of a visit, he wrote a letter to the **Romans** (A.D. 56). In this he gave the fullest exposition yet written of the great doctrines of sin, justification, and sanctification. He wanted to make sure this church in the capital of the Roman Empire was well established in the central truths of Christianity.

During Paul's two years' imprisonment at Rome (A.D. 59 to 61), he wrote the four Prison Letters. **Philemon** is a short personal note to this Christian slave owner about his runaway slave, Onesimus. **Colossians** was sent to the church meeting in this same man's house. It deals with the nature and person of Christ, a crucial question of the times. **Ephesians** was probably a circular letter. In the three oldest Greek manuscripts the words "at Ephesus" are omitted in 1:1. The letter was first sent to the mother church at Ephesus and was intended also for the other congregations in the province of Asia. **Philippians** was sent to the church in Macedonia that Paul had founded on his second journey. It is a spontaneous outpouring of joy and thanksgiving. Even in prison Paul kept in touch with his churches.

Paul probably wrote **1 Timothy** and **Titus** about A.D. 62 to 64, soon after he was released from his first Roman imprisonment. Arrested again and placed in a dungeon, the apostle wrote **2 Timothy**, warning of the apostasy of the last days. These three are called the Pastoral Letters, because they deal with pastoral problems.

b. The General Letters. Seven letters of the New Testament fall into the category of the General Letters, because they are not addressed to any particular church or individual. Unlike Paul's Letters, which are named for their destination, these are named after the writer.

James is probably the earliest. Some, in fact, would date it as early as A.D. 45, thus making it the first book of the New Testament. It probably appeared in the early 60s, with **Hebrews** appearing at about this same time (middle 60s). Hebrews is not, however, classified as a General Letter, because it is clearly addressed to specific Jewish Christians tempted to return to their old life. This great letter reminds its recipients that Jesus provides better access to God than angels, Moses, or even the old sacrificial system of Judaism.

1 Peter came in the same period, apparently written from Rome. The apostle sought to encourage the believers in times of persecution.

The genuineness of **2 Peter** has been sharply debated. Assuming the apostle as author, it would have had to have been written before A.D. 68, the year of Nero's death. Early Church tradition strongly asserts both Peter and Paul died under Nero. Second Peter speaks of the second coming of Christ.

The three letters by John will be reserved for later discussion. **Jude** is much like the second chapter of 2 Peter.

  c. The Synoptic Gospels and Acts. The four Gospels are properly placed first in the New Testament. They give us the foundations of our faith in the life, death, and resurrection of Jesus Christ. They were not, however, the first books to be written. In fact, John's Gospel was one of the last. All the Gospels were likely written sometime during the last half of the first century.

John Mark apparently wrote the Gospel of **Mark** in Rome, either in the late 50s or in A.D. 65 to 70. **Matthew** appeared a little later, perhaps about A.D. 60, or, as some prefer, in the 70s. **Luke** may be dated in the early 60s but has also been placed at about A.D. 80. **Acts,** the sequel to Luke, then appeared either about A.D. 62 or 90.

d. The Johannine Writings. It is now generally believed that the Gospel of **John**, the three letters of **John**, and **Revelation** were all written in the last decade of the first century. We do not know whether the Gospel of John or the letters of John appeared first. The Book of **Revelation**, with its picture of the new heaven and the new earth, forms a perfect conclusion to the entire divine revelation contained in the Bible.

The Gospel of John was written that readers might believe Jesus is the Messiah, the Son of God, and as a result of believing they might have life in Him (20:31). The First Letter of John was written to believers that they might know they have eternal life (5:13). The Book of Revelation gives a vision of the glorified Christ in the middle of His Church (chapter 1), messages to the seven churches of Asia (chapters 2-3), and a preview of the future (chapters 4–22).

Questions

1. Why is it important to believe in the divine inspiration of the Bible?

2. In what ways is the Bible a divine-human Book?

3. Why does the Bible give so much space to the history of Israel?

4. What books are included in the "Wisdom Literature" of the Old Testament?

5. What were the earliest books of the New Testament, and for what purpose were they written?

6. Why was the Bible written as a Book of Life rather than a Book of theology?

Its Two Preservation

The Bible is a library of sixty-six books written over a period of 1,500 years. The thirty-nine books of the Old Testament took about 1,000 years to appear (roughly 1400 to 400 B.C.). The twenty-seven books of the New Testament were written in a much shorter span of time, about fifty years (A.D. 45 to 95). Nearly forty writers were involved in producing these sixty-six books. How did these books finally come to be one volume called "The Holy Bible"?

The word "Bible" comes from the Greek plural *ta biblia*, meaning "the books," via the singular Latin term *biblia*, meaning "the book." How did "the Books" become "the Book"? This is the subject of discussion in this chapter.

The Old Testament Canon

By "canon" we mean an officially accepted list of books that are authoritative for belief and practice. The Protestant canon of the Old Testament is the same as the Hebrew canon accepted by the Jews as constituting "The Holy Scriptures." This is the complete Jewish Bible. The Roman Catholic canon of the Old Testament is longer, including fourteen books, or parts of books, that are missing in the Old Testament with which we are familiar. The Orthodox canon contains these fourteen plus three additional books. Why this difference?

a. The Hebrew Canon. The basic nucleus of the Hebrew canon is the Torah, or Law of Moses. It consists of the first five books of our Old Testament. The Sadducees of Jesus' day placed primary emphasis on this part of their sacred Scriptures. The Pharisees also assigned it great importance, as do most Jews today.

In the Hebrew Bible the first book carries the heading *bereshith*, "In the Beginning." It was the custom of the Jews to use the first Hebrew word of each book as the title.

In our Bibles the names of the first five books are taken largely from the ancient Greek translation of the Old Testament known as the Septuagint (discussed in chapter 4). *Genesis* is simply the Greek word for "beginning." *Exodus* is from the Greek *exodos*, meaning "a going out." The main event in this book is the exodus of the Israelites from Egypt. *Leviticus* is so named because it refers largely to the work of the priests, who were Levites. *Numbers* is the English equivalent of the Greek *arithmoi*, its name in the Septuagint. The book records two numberings of the people of Israel, one made at Sinai soon after they left Egypt (chapter 1) and the other in the plains of Moab just before they crossed into Canaan (chapter 26). *Deuteronomy* is composed of two Greek words, *deuteros*, "second," and *nomos*, "law." It describes the second giving of the Law of Moses. The first was to the generation of Israelites who came out of Egypt, and it occurred at Sinai. The second was to the next generation before they entered the Promised Land.

The Hebrew canon contained three divisions: (1) the Law, (2) the Prophets, (3) the Writings. The Law consisted of the five books of Moses. The Prophets were divided into the Former Prophets and the Latter Prophets, each containing four books. The Former Prophets included Joshua, Judges, Samuel, and Kings (considered as one book each). The Latter Prophets consisted of Isaiah, Jeremiah, Ezekiel, and the Twelve. In the Hebrew canon the twelve Minor Prophets were placed together and referred to as "The Book of the Twelve."

Christians usually list Joshua, Judges, Samuel, and Kings among the historical books of the Old Testament. The Jews thought of their history as prophetic history and so classified these books under the Prophets.

The third division, the Writings, included the rest of the books of our Old Testament. These were further divided into the three Poetical Books (Psalms, Proverbs, Job), the Five Rolls (Song of Songs, Ruth, Lamentations, Ecclesiastes, Esther), and the three Historical Books (Daniel, Ezra-Nehemiah, Chronicles).

One passage in the New Testament makes reference to this division. In Luke 24:44 Jesus said, "Everything must be fulfilled that is written about me in the Law of Moses, the Prophets and the Psalms." The third division, the Writings, began with the Book of Psalms. Sometimes this group as a whole was referred to as "the Psalms."

A quick count shows the "books" of the Hebrew canon totaled twenty-four. This includes all thirty-nine books in our Old Testament. Josephus, prominent Jewish historian of the first century of the Christian era, speaks of "only twenty-two books" in their sacred scriptures. Perhaps this was because there were twenty-two letters in the Hebrew alphabet. This number was achieved by combining Ruth with Judges and Lamentations with Jeremiah. Eventually Ruth and Lamentations were placed with the other short books to form the Five Rolls. Second Esdras 14:45 speaks of twenty-four books.

Perhaps one reason the Five Rolls were put together was their special use in worship. Each would consist of a single scroll. The Song of Songs was read at the Passover, Ruth at the Feast of Weeks (Pentecost), Ecclesiastes at the Feast of Tabernacles, and Esther at the Feast of Purim. Lamentations was read on the fast day commemorating the destruction of Jerusalem in 586/87 B.C.

In Hebrew Scriptures today we have 39 books. The order of the ancient Hebrew canon is preserved, beginning with Genesis and ending with 2 Chronicles. Isaiah comes after 2 Kings, and Psalms after Malachi, with Song of Songs following Job, and Daniel following Esther. Thus the threefold division of the Hebrew canon continues.

When and why did the Jews officially establish their canon of Scripture? The books of the Law were believed to possess divine authority. The individual books of the Prophets were probably accepted as sacred at the time of their appearance. We know it took some time for all the writings to be received as Scripture. The Book of Esther was disputed right down to the time of Christ. This is reflected in the fact that in the Dead Sea caves have been found fragments of every book of the Old Testament except Esther.

The situation after A.D. 70 called for official action. In that year the Temple was destroyed, along with the city of Jerusalem. This brought an end to the Jewish sacrificial system. The Sadducees, who dominated the priesthood, faded out of sight.

The Pharisees, who taught the Scriptures in the numerous synagogues, survived as the leaders. The Jews became the people of the Book. The exact limits of sacred Scripture needed to be set. There must be no doubt as to what books were accepted as having divine authority.

There was another very important factor. Christian writings began appearing—the Letters of Paul, other letters, and especially the Gospels. These were condemned and their use prohibited by adherents of Judaism.

At the Council of Jamnia, about A.D. 90, the rabbis officially fixed the limits of the Hebrew canon. Included were the thirty-nine books of the present Hebrew Bible, divided into the Law, the Prophets, and the Writings.

b. The Apocrypha. If you happen across a large old pulpit Bible and look through it, you may discover some extensive material between the Old and New Testaments. You may find fourteen books or parts of books, altogether about five-sixths as long as the New Testament. These books are called the Apocrypha.

This term means "hidden." Those who favored these books claimed they were withdrawn from common use because they contained secret wisdom. Such wisdom was known only by the initiated. Those who rejected them said they were hidden because they were spurious. Jerome (fourth century) seems to have been the first to call these books "Apocrypha."

The fourteen books are 1 and 2 Esdras, Tobit, Judith, Additions to Esther, the Wisdom of Solomon, Ecclesiasticus (also known as the Wisdom of Sirach), Baruch, Susanna, the Song of the Three Children, Bel and the Dragon, the Prayer of Manasseh, and 1 and 2 Maccabees. They were apparently written during the three centuries between 200 B.C. and A.D. 100.

In the Greek Septuagint and Latin Vulgate these books are scattered throughout the Old Testament. Martin Luther was the first to separate them. In 1534 he completed his translation of the Bible from the original Greek and Hebrew. Since the apoc-

ryphal books were not in the Hebrew Bible, he translated them last and put them by themselves between the Old and New Testaments. Myles Coverdale followed this pattern when he put out the first printed English Bible the next year, 1535. All the Protestant English Bibles did the same, down to and including the King James Version (1611). The Catholic and Orthodox Bibles still have the Apocrypha scattered throughout the Old Testament, as in the Latin Vulgate.

The Bibles with which Protestant Christians are most familiar today do not have the apocryphal books in them at all. If they were in the original King James Version, how and when were they omitted?

In the Prologue of the Great Bible of 1539, Jerome is credited with suggesting the Apocrypha was edifying but not authoritative. The Geneva Bible of 1560 went further, suggesting they were not to be used for deciding doctrine. The Apocrypha was useful for knowledge of history and instruction in godly living. The Bishops' Bible (1568) issued no such warning. Since the King James Version (1611) was a revision of the Bishops' Bible, it simply gave the heading "Apocrypha," without any disparaging note. In fact, one of the men who produced the King James Version became Archbishop of Canterbury. He issued a decree that anyone who published the English Bible without the Apocrypha should be imprisoned for a year!

The Puritans "persecuted the Apocrypha," as Frederick Kenyon aptly observes. As far back as 1590 some copies of their Geneva Bible began to appear without the apocryphal books. By 1629 the same was happening to the King James Version, under Puritan influence.

The official view of the Church of England is stated in its Thirty-nine Articles. After speaking of the "canonical books" it goes on to say, "And the other Books (as Jerome saith) the Church doth read for example of life and instruction of manners; but yet doth it not apply them to establish any doctrine."

In the early nineteenth century action was taken to exclude the apocryphal books. The National Bible Society of Scotland took this position: If these books are not the inspired Word of God, money should not be wasted in printing them as part of the Bible. It petitioned the British and Foreign Bible Society, which voted in 1827 not to use any of its funds in publishing the Apocrypha. From that time most copies of the King James Version omitted these books.

The *English Revised Version* came out in 1885 without the Apocrypha but did publish the latter in 1894. Similarly, the *Revised Standard Version* appeared in 1952 with no Apocrypha. At the request of the General Convention of the Protestant Episcopal Church in that year, it made up for this deficiency by publishing a translation of the Apocrypha in 1965. Meanwhile Professor Edgar J. Goodspeed of the University of Chicago popularized the Apocrypha among many Protestants by having his excellent translation included in *An American Translation: The Complete Bible* (1939). The Apocrypha is now available in various modern translations. It can be found in certain editions of the *New English Bible*, the *New Revised Standard Version*, the *English Standard Version*, the *Revised English Bible*, and even the King James Version. One might say the Apocrypha is "in" again, at least for some Protestants.

What should be our attitude toward the Apocrypha? In the first place, we must recognize there is much material of historical and religious value. But we agree with sound Protestant opinion of four hundred years: These books are not a part of the inspired, authoritative Word of God. As such we believe they have no place in the Bible but should be studied separately.

Since most Protestants are not familiar with the Apocrypha, a brief overview of each book may be in order. Since the Roman Catholic and Orthodox churches officially hold these books to be part of the inspired, authoritative Bible, we need to know more about them.

First Esdras (about 150 B.C.) tells of the restoration of the Jews to Palestine after the Babylonian exile. It draws much from Chronicles, Ezra, and Nehemiah. In addition, the author has added much legendary material.

The most interesting item is the Story of the Three Guardsmen. They were debating what was the strongest thing in the world. One said, "Wine"; another, "the King"; the third, "Woman and Truth." They put these three answers under the king's pillow. When he awoke he required the three men to defend their answers. The unanimous decision was "Truth is greatly and supremely strong." Because Zerubbabel had given this answer, he was allowed, as a reward, to rebuild the Temple at Jerusalem.

Second Esdras (A.D. 100-200) is a collection of three apocalyptic works containing seven visions reportedly from Ezra the scribe. Martin Luther was so confused by these visions that he is said to have thrown the book into the Elbe River.

Tobit (early second century B.C.) is a short novel. Strongly Pharisaic in tone, it emphasizes the Law, clean foods, ceremonial washings, charity, fasting, and prayer. It is clearly unscriptural in its statement that almsgiving atones for sin.

Judith (late second century B.C.) is also fictitious and Pharisaic. The heroine of this novel is Judith, a beautiful Jewish widow. When her city was besieged she took her maid, together with clean Jewish food, and went out to the tent of the attacking general. He was taken by her beauty and gave her a place in his tent. Fortunately, he had imbibed too freely and sank into a drunken stupor. Judith took his sword and cut off his head. Then she and her maid left the camp, taking his head in their provision bag. It was hung on the wall of a nearby city, and the leaderless Assyrian army was defeated.

Additions to Esther (about 100 B.C.) make up for the absence of overt spiritual statements in that book. Esther stands alone among the books of the Old Testament in having no mention of God. We are told that Esther and Mordecai fasted. No mention of prayer, however, is made. To compensate for this lack, the Additions have long prayers attributed to these two. Several letters supposedly written by Artaxerxes are also included.

The Wisdom of Solomon (about A.D. 40) was written to keep the Jews from falling into skepticism, materialism, and idolatry. As in Proverbs, Wisdom is personified. There are many noble sentiments expressed in this book.

Ecclesiasticus, or Wisdom of Sirach (about 180 B.C.), shows a high level of religious wisdom, somewhat like the canonical Book of Proverbs. It also contains much practical advice. For instance, on the subject of after-dinner speeches it says, "Speak concisely; say much in few words; act like a man who knows more than he says" (32:8).

In his sermons John Wesley quotes several times from the Book of Ecclesiasticus. It is still widely used in Anglican circles.

Baruch (about 150 B.C. or A.D. 100) was reportedly written by Baruch, the scribe of Jeremiah, in 582 B.C., though it seems to come from much later. It apparently attempts to interpret the destruction of Jerusalem in either 587/586 B.C. or A.D. 70. The book urges the Jews not to revolt again and to submit to the emperor. The sixth chapter of Baruch contains the so-called Letter of Jeremiah, with its strong warning against idolatry.

Our Book of Daniel contains twelve chapters. In the first century before Christ a thirteenth chapter was added, the story of *Susanna*. She was the beautiful wife of a leading Jew in Babylon falsely accused of infidelity. Because of Daniel's wisdom she was rescued. He asked each of her accusers separately under which tree in the garden they found Susanna with a lover. When they gave different answers, they were put to death, and Susanna was saved.

Bel and the Dragon was added at about the same time and called chapter 14 of Daniel. Its main purpose was to show the folly of idolatry. It really contains two stories.

In the first, King Cyrus asked Daniel why he did not worship Bel, since that deity showed his greatness by daily consuming much flour and oil and many sheep. Daniel scattered ashes on the floor of the Temple where food had been placed that evening. In the morning Daniel showed the king the footprints of the priests and their families who had entered secretly under the table and consumed the food. The priests were slain and the temple destroyed.

The story of the Dragon is just as obviously legendary in character. Along with Tobit, Judith, and Susanna, these stories may be classified as Jewish fiction. They have little if any religious value.

The *Song of the Three Hebrew Children* follows Daniel 3:23 in the Septuagint and the Vulgate. It describes what happened to Shadrach, Meshach, and Abednego inside the fiery furnace. Borrowing heavily from Psalm 148, it is antiphonal, like Psalm 136. The refrain "Sing praise to him and greatly exalt him forever" appears thirty-two times.

The *Prayer of Manasseh* was composed in Maccabean times (second century B.C.) or later as the supposed prayer of Manasseh, the wicked king of Judah. It was obviously suggested by the statement in 2 Chronicles 33:19—"His prayer and how God was moved by his entreaty . . . all are written in the records of the seers." This prayer is not found otherwise in the Bible and is likely legendary.

First Maccabees (first century B.C.) is perhaps the most valuable book in the Apocrypha. It describes the exploits of three Maccabean brothers—Judas, Jonathan, and Simon—during the Jewish revolt against the Seleucid Empire in 167-164 B.C. Along with Josephus, it is our most important source for this crucial, exciting period in Jewish history.

Second Maccabees (same time) is not a sequel to 1 Maccabees. It is a parallel account, treating only the victories of Judas Maccabaeus. It is generally thought to be more legendary than 1 Maccabees.

The New Testament Canon

At about A.D. 140 in Rome, a heretic named Marcion adopted his own New Testament canon. It contained ten letters of Paul (excluding the Pastorals) and a mutilated Gospel of Luke (first two chapters missing). He rejected the entire Old Testament. To counteract his influence, it was necessary for the orthodox Christian Church to fix the limits of its canon.

At the other extreme from Marcion, many churches in the East (for example, Alexandria, Egypt) were reading certain books of the New Testament Apocrypha in their public services. A fifth-century manuscript of the Bible, Alexandrinus, has the First Letter of Clement of Rome attached to it. The Letter of Barnabas and the Shepherd of Hermas (both second-century books) are found at the end of Sinaiticus, a fourth-century manuscript of the Bible. Clearly a decision needed to be made as to exactly what books were to be included in the canon.

A third factor was the edict of Diocletian, in A.D. 303, demanding the destruction of all sacred books of Christianity. Would Christians want to risk their lives by having in their possession a religious book that was not really inspired by God?

Most scholars believe the only genuine Christian writing we have from the first century, outside the New Testament, is Clement of Rome's First Letter, written about A.D. 95. It contains references to Matthew, Romans, and 1 Corinthians, along with allusions to Hebrews.

The earliest church fathers of the second century, such as Ignatius and Polycarp, show a wide acquaintance with Paul's letters, some of the Gospels, and 1 Peter and 1 John. This use of our New Testament books increased steadily down through the middle of that century. For instance, Justin Martyr (A.D. 150) shows knowledge of the four Gospels, Acts, several of Paul's letters, Hebrews, 1 Peter, and Revelation. By the end of the second century it is clear Irenaeus in Gaul (France), Clement of Alexandria (Egypt), and Tertullian of Carthage (North Africa) all had essentially the same New Testament as we have today.

During the third century there was considerable dispute about the canonicity of seven of our New Testament books. These were Hebrews, James, 2 Peter, 2 and 3 John, Jude, and Revelation. This uncertainty continued on into the fourth century. The first exact list of our twenty-seven books is found in the Easter letter of Athanasius, in A.D. 367. Finally, near the close of the fourth century, in A.D. 397, the Council of Carthage decreed that only "canonical" books should be read in the churches. It then proceeded to list exactly the twenty-seven books of our New Testament. From that day to this the canon of the New Testament has remained the same for the Roman Catholic and Orthodox churches and has been the Protestant canon since the Reformation. We believe the Holy Spirit led in the selections made.

Questions

1. What is the advantage of having the Bible written by many different people rather than by one person? (See Ephesians 3:18.)

2. In what ways is the Bible a library of books? In what way is it "the Book"?

3. What were the three divisions of the Hebrew canon, and which books were included in each division?

4. What is the difference between the Catholic and Protestant Old Testaments, and what is the reason for this?

5. Why did the Early Church form a canon of the New Testament?

6. When was the canon finalized officially?

Its **Three** Transmission

We do not have the original copy of a single book of the Bible. This fact alone demands careful investigation of the text of both Old and New Testaments. Are we justified in believing that we have a reliably authentic copy of each of the sixty-six books of the sacred canon?

The Old Testament Text

We are fortunate to live in the age of archaeological discoveries. Time was when some scholars asserted Moses could not have written the Pentateuch because the art of writing was unknown at that early date (about 1400 B.C.). As in many other cases, archaeology has silenced this argument forever. At Ur and Nippur, in Mesopotamia, thousands of clay tablets have been dug up, going back as far as 2100 B.C. We have tablets from Abraham's hometown inscribed at the very time he lived there—half a millennium before Moses. From the other great center of earliest civilization, the Nile valley, we have papyrus manuscripts from before 2000 B.C. Some contain texts that claim to have been written originally before 3000 B.C. It is evident that writing is an ancient art.

In 1929 a startling discovery was made at the site of the ancient city of Ugarit, on the northwest coast of Syria. Archaeological excavations revealed a large building that housed a library, a scribes' school, and the home of the chief priest of the local cult. In the library were found hundreds of tablets written in strange script. Later excavations (1952-53) unearthed the ancient Ugaritic alphabet, composed of thirty letters. The tablet on which it is written is thought to have come from the fourteenth century B.C., near the time of Moses. The Ugaritic language is Semitic, a sister language to Hebrew. Since this discovery many commentaries make use of parallels in Ugaritic literature as a help in understanding the meaning of Hebrew terms.

"Moses was educated in all the wisdom of the Egyptians" (Acts 7:22), having received a royal education in the literature of ancient Egypt. When the Israelites under Joshua entered the land of Canaan, they found an alphabet and a large body of religious literature in a Semitic language. The physical tools were at hand for writing the Old Testament.

As to writing materials, the Egyptians used leather scrolls at an early time. Specimens from about 2000 B.C have been discovered. The later Jewish Talmud required all copies of the Law to be written on skins and in roll form. This rule is still in force.

a. The Pre-Masoretic Text. Humanly speaking, it is impossible for anyone to copy by hand a document as long as the prophecy of Isaiah without making some mistakes. We must remember that all the copies of the books of the Old and New Testaments were made by hand until the middle of the fifteenth century (A.D. 1456). Some had been copied for nearly 3,000 years and all of them for well over 1,000 years. Not until the modern age of printing was it possible to produce large numbers of copies of a book, all of them exactly the same.

It is not surprising to find some differences in the text of the Old Testament manuscripts. We may be thankful, however, for the fact the Hebrew scribes were very careful in copying sacred Scriptures. They realized this was a serious responsibility. R. K. Harrison says, "In the immediate pre-Christian period the Jewish authorities gave a great deal of thought to the preservation of the Old Testament text in as pure a form as possible, a concern prompted as much by the existence of manuscript variants as by differences between the Hebrew and LXX texts."[1] They tried to correct errors that crept into the text through centuries of copying manuscripts from one generation to another.

In the second century of the Christian era Rabbi Aqiba sought to fix the text with exactness. He is credited with saying that "the accurate transmission (*masoreth*) of the text is a fence for the Torah."[2] For the purpose of closer study, the scribes divided the Hebrew text into verses.

b. The Masoretic Text. Near the beginning of the sixth century the work of the scribes in copying the Old Testament manuscripts was taken over by the Masoretes, who functioned about A.D. 500 to 1000. They worked with meticulous care, counting the number of verses, words, and even letters in each book of the Old Testament. They went so far as even to identify the middle letter of each book. By counting the letters they made sure not one had been added or left out. This meant the text was now copied with greater accuracy than ever before.

The contribution for which the Masoretes are most famous is the addition of vowel points. The Hebrew alphabet consists of consonants only. It is as if we were to write the first verse of

Genesis as follows (in Hebrews the articles and prepositions are attached to the nouns):

NTHBGNNNGGDCRTDTHHVNNDTHRTH

It is obvious a combination of three consonants—the most frequent number for a Hebrew root—could yield several different words, depending on what vowels were inserted between the consonants. For example, in English, *l-v-d* could be *lived, loved,* or *livid.* Of course, the context would usually, but not always, indicate which of these it would be.

Another important factor should be taken into consideration. Apparently all reading in ancient times was done aloud. The Scriptures were read aloud each Sabbath in the synagogues, and earlier in the Temple and Tabernacle. The scribes read the Word of God aloud each day. At that time the method of instruction in the schoolroom was for the teacher to read a sentence from a scroll and his pupils to repeat it after him. In this way the people were familiar with the sound as well as the sense.

Across the centuries it was inevitable that there would arise some differences of opinion as to how specific words should be pronounced. Scribes made mistakes in copying the consonants. What was really the traditional text?

The Masoretes—from *masorah,* "tradition"—undertook the task of correcting and standardizing the text. To ensure accuracy of pronunciation, it was necessary to indicate the vowel sounds. To the consonantal text, copied for hundreds of years, the Masoretes added "vowel points." These were combinations of dots and lines under, within or above the consonants. The resulting text is called the Masoretic text. It is the standard text of the Hebrew Old Testament studied today. With the care the Masoretes gave to copying the Scriptures, this text comes down to us from the Middle Ages with little change. Since the fifteenth century it has been fixed solidly in print.

c. The Dead Sea Scrolls. Before 1947 the oldest Hebrew manuscript we had was from about the beginning of the tenth century (A.D. 900). How would we know this represented the Hebrew text in use in the days of Christ, to say nothing of Old Testament times? No certain answer could be given to this disturbing question.

Through archaeological research, the answer finally came. In 1947 a complete manuscript of the Hebrew text of Isaiah was found. Paleographers date it around 125 B.C. It is 1,000 years older than the oldest copy of Isaiah known to that time.

The story of this discovery is one of the most fascinating tales of modern times. In February or March of 1947 a Bedouin shepherd boy named Muhammad was searching for a lost goat. He tossed a stone into a hole in a cliff on the west side of the Dead Sea, about eight miles south of Jericho. To his surprise, he heard the sound of shattering pottery. Investigating, he discovered an amazing sight. On the floor of the cave were several large jars containing leather scrolls, wrapped in linen cloth. Because the jars were carefully sealed, the scrolls had been preserved in excellent condition for nearly 1,900 years. They were evidently placed there in A.D. 68.

When the scrolls were first discovered, virtually no publicity was given to them. In November 1947, two days after Professor Sukenik of the Hebrew University purchased three scrolls and two jars from the cave, he wrote in his diary, "It may be that this is one of the greatest finds ever made in Palestine, a find we never so much as hoped for." These significant words were not published at the time.

The archbishop of the Syrian Orthodox Monastery at Jerusalem bought five of the scrolls found in Dead Sea Cave 1. Fortunately, in February 1948, the archbishop, who could not read Hebrew, phoned the American School of Oriental Research in

Jerusalem about the scrolls. The acting director of the school was a young scholar named John Trever, who was an excellent amateur photographer. With dedicated labor he photographed each column of the Isaiah scroll, which is twenty-four feet long and ten inches high. He developed the plates and sent a few prints by airmail to W. F. Albright of Johns Hopkins University. Albright was widely recognized as the dean of American biblical archaeologists. Albright wrote back, "My heartiest congratulations on the greatest manuscript discovery of modern times! . . . What an absolutely incredible find! And there can happily not be the slightest doubt in the world about the genuineness of the manuscript." He dated it about 100 B.C.

Among the other manuscripts found in Cave 1 were a commentary on Habakkuk and a "Rule of the Community." This was a manual of discipline for the religious community. In 1950-51 the American Schools of Oriental Research published these two, together with the Isaiah scroll. In 1954 the Hebrew University published three other manuscripts from Cave 1, including a document called "The War Between the Children of Light and the Children of Darkness." This terminology reminds us of John's Gospel and First Letter.

Archaeologists have investigated numerous caves around the Dead Sea since the initial find. Portions of over eight hundred documents have been discovered. In addition to the contents of Cave 1, the most valuable finds were in Caves 4 and 11. Cave 4 yielded thousands of fragments, including parts of every Old Testament book except Esther. Fragments of the Apocrypha were also found. The favorite biblical books of the community were Genesis, Deuteronomy, the Psalms, and Isaiah. These are doubtless the very four that would be chosen from the Old Testament by thoughtful Christians today.

Near these caves archaeologists uncovered the ruins of an ancient fortified monastery. One can now walk through this building and view the various rooms. The most interesting is the building many scholars call the Scriptorium, where scribes may have copied manuscripts. Here were found a long, narrow table, a bench, and two inkwells. There was also an assembly hall, about seventy-five by fifteen feet in size. The walls of the monastery enclosed a pottery—where the cave jars were probably made—a forge, a grain mill, a bakery, and a laundry.

The place is known today as Qumran. It is generally agreed the Qumran community belonged to a Jewish sect called the Essenes. In A.D. 68, two years before the destruction of Jerusalem, the Roman army burned the monastery. As the enemy approached, Essene scribes apparently hid valuable manuscripts in the nearby caves so they would not be found or destroyed. Today we can be thankful they took this precaution.

The biblical scrolls found at Qumran have been dated from 200 B.C. to A.D. 68. The Isaiah scroll, as noted earelier, is dated about 125 B.C., 1,000 years earlier than the oldest previously known manuscript of that book. A replica of this scroll, along with other scrolls and fragments, are on display in the Book of the Shrine in Jerusalem. This museum was built especially for the Dead Sea Scrolls. Portions of the collection are allowed to go on tour to other museums throughout the world from time to time. Some fragments still remain in the hands of scholars to be studied and published.

The crucial question immediately coming to mind is this: How does its text compare with the Masoretic text from the Middle Ages? The answer is reassuring. It agrees closely. As expected, there are minor variations. Translators of the *Revised Standard Version* (1952), one of the first translations to make use of the new discovery, accepted about fourteen variant readings. They are identified by footnotes saying, "one ancient MS." Nearly every translation since the RSV has relied upon the Dead Sea Scrolls for improved readings of the Hebrew text. Some manuscripts, especially from Cave 4, are often closer to the Septuagint than to the Masoretic text. The Dead Sea Scrolls have provided scholars with important information for establishing a more exact text of the Old Testament.

The New Testament Text

"There are thousands of variant readings in the Greek New Testament." This statement, found some years ago in a popular magazine and frequently repeated by some people, is technically true. The impression given in the context of the article, however, was morally untrue. The author probably left most of his readers somewhat shattered with the feeling that the Greek text of the New Testament must be in a state of utter chaos.

Such, of course, is not the case at all. The vast majority of these variations are differences in spelling or grammatical form. These matters have no significance whatever for the meaning of the text.

In 1853 two Cambridge scholars, B. F. Westcott and F. J. A. Hort, set out to construct an accurate text of the New Testament based on the best Greek manuscripts. After twenty years of devoted work, they published *The New Testament in the Original*

Greek (1881), a standard work used by generations of students of the Greek New Testament.

Not so well known is Volume II, "Introduction and Appendix," actually written by Hort. Of the Greek text of the New Testament, Hort says, "The proportion of words virtually accepted on all hands as raised above doubt is very great, not less, on a rough computation, than seven eights of the whole." He goes on to say, "Setting aside differences of orthography (spelling, etc.), the words in our opinion still subject to doubt only make up about one sixtieth of the whole New Testament." He then asserts, "The amount of what can in any sense be called substantial variation is but a small fraction of the whole residuary variation, and can hardly form more than a thousandth part of the entire text."[3]

Many scholars agree that Hort's last statement is a bit too optimistic. Nevertheless, it underscores the basic reliability of the Greek text of the New Testament as we now have it.

a. Kinds of Errors. No two manuscripts of the Greek New Testament are exactly alike. Humanly speaking, this is unavoidable. It would be nearly impossible for two people to copy by hand the entire Greek text of the New Testament without making mistakes. The books of the New Testament were all copied by hand for over 1,000 years before the age of printing began in the middle of the fifteenth century.

There are two main classes of unintentional mistakes made by copyists. These are errors of the eye and errors of the ear.

1. Errors of the eye. Such mistakes will almost inevitably be made by anyone who copies a long document. The problem is compounded in the case of the Greek New Testament by several factors.

In the older Greek manuscripts there are not only no chapter and verse divisions and no separation into sentences but also no separation between words. It is as if we should write the first verse of Luke's Gospel as follows:

FORASMUCHASMANYHAVETAKENINHAN
DTOSETFORTHINORDERADECLARATION
OFTHOSETHINGSWHICHAREMOSTS
URELYBELIEVEDAMONGUS

And so it goes on, line after line, column after column, through a whole book of the New Testament. When a person was copying one manuscript from another, he might make a wrong division between words. Of course, he would usually be aware of this and correct the mistake. ISAWABUNDANCEONTHET-ABLE could be taken as "I saw a bun dance on the table" or "I saw abundance on the table." Mistakes of this type are found in later Greek manuscripts (e.g., fifteenth century), when separation between words was introduced.

In the second place, the oldest Greek manuscripts commonly use abbreviations for such words as "God," "Christ," "Jesus," and "Son," with an overhead line connecting the first and last letters. For example, "Christ" appears as "XY," "Jesus" as "IC," "Son" as "YC," each with a line overhead. It is obvious it would be easier to confuse these abbreviations than it would be if the words were written out in full.

A third type of error is still very common today—the omission of a line when two consecutive lines begin or end with the same word. One who frequently prepares copy for word processing soon learns to watch for this. A similar situation is the omission or addition of similar clauses, or even sentences.

2. *Errors of the ear.* As we have seen, a scribe copying one manuscript from another could make errors of the eye. Sometimes a man would sit at a table, slowly reading aloud a manuscript to a group of scribes seated in front of him. This was the

only kind of publishing house in those days. Usually not more than forty scribes would be involved at a time.

In the case of a group copying from dictation, errors of the ear were bound to occur. This would happen today in such copying of English manuscripts. There are many words sounding alike but different in spelling and meaning. One scribe would hear it one way; another would take it a different way.

To compound the situation, most of the vowels and diphthongs in the Greek of that day, as in modern Greek, were pronounced alike, sounding like our long "e." I once sat in a Greek prayer meeting in Athens where I would not have been able to follow the Scripture reading at all if I had not held a Greek Testament in my hand. In a Greek-speaking Church of the Nazarene in Sydney, Australia, I had a similar experience. When I got up to preach, I announced, "Now I'm going to read the pastor's scripture lesson the way we pronounce it." I proceeded to do so, much to the enjoyment of the audience!

b. Abundance of Manuscripts. Lest the reader feel disturbed by the picture we have just painted, we hasten to say that most of these errors can be quickly spotted and eliminated. We now have over 5,000 manuscripts of the Greek New Testament, in whole or in part. By careful comparison we can eliminate most mistakes made in copying. In cases where we cannot be absolutely certain—and there are such situations—we can be sure not one of these variant readings adversely affects a single doctrine of our Christian faith.

1. Papyri. The common writing material of the first century was papyrus, from which we get our term "paper." It was made by taking stalks from the papyrus plant and slicing the pith into thin strips. Two layers of these strips were placed together crosswise, with glue between, and allowed to dry. The resulting material was brittle and fragile. It is usually assumed all the New

Testament was written on papyrus, with the possible exception of the four Gospels and Acts. This is the basic reason no original copies have survived.

Papyri were unknown in modern times until 1778, when an earthenware pot containing fifty papyrus rolls was discovered in Egypt. The first major discovery of Greek papyri took place in 1897. Bernard Grenfell and Arthur Hunt of England were excavating near the village of Oxyrhynchus, about one hundred twenty miles south of Cairo. In the rubbish mounds of the town they discovered much papyrus material. Most of it was secular papers and documents. This find gave new light to the meaning of many New Testament words.

An example may be seen in the repeated statement of Jesus "They have their reward" (Matthew 6:2, 5, 16). The regular Greek word for "have" in the New Testament is *echo*. Here we find the compound *apecho*. The rubbish heaps of Egypt disclosed hundreds of formal receipts, all of them containing this word. Modern translations include the more adequate rendering, "They have received their reward." The meaning of Jesus' words is clear. Those who practice their religion in order to get the praise of men have a receipt, "Paid in full." They can claim no further reward in the next life. We have to decide whether eternal dividends are worth sacrificing on the altar of earthly glory.

Papyrus manuscripts of the Greek New Testament are a more recent discovery. The largest and most important of them have come to light since 1930. The Chester Beatty Papyri (Dublin, Ireland) include three documents from the third century—one of the four Gospels and Acts, very incomplete; another of the Pauline letters, nearly complete; and a third of Revelation, the middle part. These are numbered Papyrus 45, 46, and 47.

Since then, the outstanding manuscripts have been the Bodmer Papyri (Geneva, Switzerland), discovered and edited in the

1950s and 1960s. Papyrus 66 of John's Gospel is thought to have come from around A.D. 200. Papyrus 72 has the earliest known text of Jude, 1 Peter, and 2 Peter. This is also from the third century. Another manuscript from the third century is Papyrus 75, containing much of the Gospels of Luke and John.

The oldest known portion of the New Testament is sometimes called "Rylands Fragment" but officially labeled Papyrus 52. It contains part of John 18 and is dated to A.D. 125. This was only about thirty years after the Gospel was originally written. Another fragment of John, Papyri 90, is also dated in the second century, toward the latter part of it.

Only about 120 New Testament papyrus manuscripts have been found to date. They are of great importance, since they reach back to the second and third centuries, only decades after the final words of the New Testament were completed.

2. *Uncials.* There are about three hundred uncial manuscripts extant, reaching from the third to eleventh centuries. These are written in large block letters and are second in importance only to the papyri.

We have two great uncial Bibles from the fourth century, the Vaticanus and Sinaiticus. The former, as the name suggests, is in the Vatican Library at Rome. The second gets its name from the fact it was found on Mount Sinai. Today it can be seen in the British Museum in London. The last part of the New Testament section of Vaticanus is broken off and lost. The Sinaiticus has a complete New Testament.

The story of the discovery of the Sinaiticus manuscript may serve to show something of the labor expended in seeking to recover the oldest Greek text. In 1844 Constantine Tischendorf made a trip to the Middle East in search of ancient manuscripts. He worked in the library of the monastery of St. Catherine at Mount Sinai, reputed to be the oldest Christian monastery in the world.

Noticing some stray leather pages of manuscript lying in a wastebasket, he took a look at them. To his astonishment, he found they were leaves of the oldest Greek Bible he had ever seen. He rescued forty-three of these leaves, which the monks let him have. They told him they had already burned the contents of two baskets!

After extracting a promise from them that they would not destroy any more, he took the forty-three leaves with him to Leipzig. Returning to the monastery in 1853, he looked in vain for the rest of the manuscript. The monks would tell him nothing.

In 1859 he decided to make another attempt, sponsored by the czar of Russia, patron of the Greek Orthodox Church. After fruitless days at the monastery of St. Catherine, he gave orders to his camel drivers to be ready to leave for Cairo the next morning.

That evening the steward of the monastery invited Tischendorf to his room to see an old copy of the Septuagint. Soon the German scholar had in his hands a heap of loose leaves wrapped in a red cloth. To his astonishment, he discovered it was the very manuscript from which had come the forty-three leaves acquired fifteen years earlier. At last his eager search had been rewarded.

Concealing feelings of joy, Tischendorf casually asked if he might take the manuscript to his room to examine it further. He stayed up all night, copying part of it, since he had no assurance he could take it with him.

In the morning he tried in vain to purchase it. He asked permission to take it to Cairo to study, but the monk in charge of the library objected. When he got to Cairo he persuaded the superior of the monastery there to send to Sinai for the manuscript. Tischendorf was allowed to copy it a few sheets at a time.

A new archbishop was elected at this time. The monks had a candidate whom they wanted to be elected. Tischendorf suggested they present the precious manuscript to the czar of Russia, the protector of the Greek church, to gain his support for their candidate. And so it was done. In addition to a favorable election, the monks received a present of money from the czar, while the manuscript was safely deposited in St. Petersburg.

In 1933 the Soviet government of Russia, caring little for a Bible and needing cash, offered to sell Codex Sinaiticus. It was purchased by the British Museum for half a million dollars, the highest price ever paid for a book up to that time.

In the United States, the oldest Greek manuscript of the four Gospels is Washingtoniensis (W), so called because it is in the Smithsonian Institution in Washington. It comes from the late fourth or early fifth century. There are several other important uncials from the fifth century (A, C, D), but most of the uncials come from later centuries.

3. *Minuscules.* From the ninth century to the fifteenth century—when printing began—we have more than 2,750 minuscule or cursive manuscripts. These are written in a small, running script. They contain the medieval Greek text of the New Testament, which is late and inferior.

With such an abundance of manuscript materials at our disposal, we can rest assured we have ample means for arriving at a close approximation of the original Greek text of the New Testament.

Questions

1. What do we mean by the "Masoretic" text of the Old Testament?

2. When were the Dead Sea Scrolls discovered, and what is their value for Old Testament studies?

3. What is the reason there are variant readings in Greek manuscripts of the New Testament?

4. What is the difference between errors of the eye and errors of the ear?

5. What is the importance of textual criticism of the New Testament?

6. Why may we feel confident that we have a reliable Greek text of the New Testament?

Its Four Translation

Over the centuries the Bible has been translated into many languages. Wherever God's message of salvation found roots, people strove to make his Word available in the local language. At times, though, these translations were opposed.

The first translations of the Hebrew Scriptures were in Aramaic and Greek. Later, Christians rendered both Old and New Testaments into Latin and Syriac. During the early centuries of Christianity many other versions emerged, such as Coptic (Egyptian), Gothic, Armenian, Ethiopic, and later, Arabic. Eventually the Bible was translated into English.

Aramaic Targums

After the Babylonian captivity many Jews could not understand the Hebrew Scriptures when they were read in public services. Most Jews at that time did not use Hebrew on a daily basis; they spoke Aramaic. Therefore, after the reading of each verse of the Law in Hebrew, an Aramaic paraphrase was given. In the case of the Prophets, the Aramaic translation came after each three verses. This custom may have begun as early as the time of Ezra (Nehemiah 8:8).

These paraphrases are known as the Aramaic Targums. At first these were simply oral paraphrases. As time went by, they became more elaborate, taking on the nature of explanations, even theological interpretations. Gradually they became fixed in form and were reduced to writing during the Christian era. Originating in Palestine, many of them were edited in Babylonia in the early Middle Ages.

Soon after the time of Christ the Samaritan Pentateuch (an alternate version of the first five books of the Bible written in Samaritan characters) was translated into the Aramaic dialect used by the Samaritans. This is called the Samaritan Targum.

Greek Versions

It may be well to define the word "version" before proceeding further. A version means a translation. Since the Old Testament was written in Hebrew, we cannot speak of a Hebrew version of the Old Testament. Similarly, we cannot talk about a Greek version of the New Testament. But we can speak of a Greek version of the Old Testament or a Latin version of the New Testament.

a. The Septuagint. The earliest translation of the Hebrew Bible (our Old Testament) is called the Septuagint. It is often designated by the Roman numerals LXX, since "septuagint" is the Latin word for "seventy." This name is due to a false tradition, based on the so-called Letter of Aristeas, that there were about seventy translators.

This letter claims to be written by an official in the court of Ptolemy Philadelphus, ruler of Egypt (285 to 247 B.C.). It tells how the emperor wanted to have in the royal library at Alexandria a copy of all the books of that day. He sent a request to the high priest in Jerusalem, asking for seventy-two capable men (six from each tribe) to translate the Law of Moses into Greek. After a royal welcome at the Alexandrian court, the seventy-two men worked on an island in seclusion, completing the translation in seventy-two days.

Later, this legendary account was further exaggerated. Philo, the Jewish philosopher at Alexandria (30 B.C. to A.D. 45), said the translators worked independently. When each finished the complete translation, the seventy-two results were identical. Anyone familiar with translation work knows this is utterly preposterous. A later writer, Epiphanius, claimed the entire Old Testament (including the Apocrypha) was completed at the same time. As we have seen, though, the apocryphal books were all written at a later date.

What are the facts? It is generally agreed that the five books of Moses were translated around the middle of the third century B.C., and the rest of the Old Testament was translated into Greek during the following two centuries (250 to 50 B.C.). Strictly speaking, the term "Septuagint" should be applied only to the Greek translation of the Pentateuch. For centuries, however, it has been applied to the entire Greek Old Testament, and so we follow that custom. Many scholars today like to refer to these early translations simply as the Old Greek.

We have noted that the Hebrew alphabet has only consonants. Consequently, the Hebrew text of the Old Testament is shorter than the Greek translation, since the Greek alphabet includes vowels. As a result, the books of Samuel, Kings, and Chronicles were too long to go on a single scroll. In the Septuagint they were divided into 1 and 2 Samuel, 1 and 2 Kings, 1 and 2 Chronicles, as we have them today in our Bibles. In the Septuagint, 1 and 2 Samuel were named 1 and 2 Kings, while our 1 and 2 Kings were called 3 and 4 Kings. This was carried over into the Latin Vulgate and into Catholic English Bibles.

Since a majority of Old Testament quotations in the New Testament are from the Septuagint, this version has great significance for us. In addition to actual quotation, much of the terminology of the Greek New Testament has its basis in the Septuagint.

The fifteenth century was an outstanding one in history. In 1492 Columbus made his famous voyage that opened up the New World of the Western Hemisphere for the spread of Christianity. Almost four decades earlier, in 1453, the Turks captured Constantinople, bringing to an end the eastern Roman Empire. Greek scholars fled to Italy, taking along with them Greek manuscripts. This sparked the Renaissance, which started in the fourteenth century. It paved the way for the Protestant Reformation of the sixteenth century. Up to this time, all education in Western Europe was in Latin. Now students began studying Greek. With the advent of printing (about 1456), this new learning was widely disseminated. These influences, taken together, mark the change from Medieval to modern times.

For the next few centuries Christian scholars sought to understand the Greek New Testament on the basis of classical Greek. The discovery of large amounts of papyri from the time of Christ added a new dimension to the study of New Testament Greek. This is reflected in lexicons and reference works written during the twentieth century. It is increasingly recognized that the single most important source for understanding the New Testament is the Septuagint Old Testament. This was the Bible used by writers of the New Testament and read by earliest Christians.

b. Later Greek Versions. More and more the Septuagint became known in the first century as the Bible of Christians. From it they derived Messianic proof texts and arguments against Judaism. In spite of the fact the Septuagint was popular among Greek-speaking Jews of the Diaspora, it was felt new Greek translations must be made.

There were three of these. The first was that of Aquila, a proselyte of Pontus (an ancient Roman province in modern Turkey). In A.D. 128 he produced a slavishly literal translation of the Hebrew text. At about the same time Theodotian revised the Septuagint. He employed a careful comparison of the Hebrew text. Toward the end of the second century Symmachus made a third translation. It was actually a paraphrase in elegant style.

Latin Versions

a. Old Latin. All the Latin versions of both the Old and New Testaments made before Jerome's revision at the end of the fourth century are known as the Old Latin versions. Apparently the first was produced in North Africa in the latter part of the second century. (It was at this time that Tertullian of North Africa became the first Church father

to write in Latin.) The Old Testament was translated from the Septuagint, not the Hebrew, while the New Testament was done from the original Greek.

In the third century several Old Latin versions were circulating in Italy, Gaul (France), and Spain. Many of these were in crude vernacular style, instead of the literary language of that day. This is probably what led Augustine to say, "In the early days of the faith, every man who happened to gain possession of the Greek manuscript and who imagined that he had any facility in both languages (however slight that may be) dared to make a translation."[1]

b. The Vulgate. It was probably in A.D. 382 that Pope Damasus requested Eusebius Hieronymus, known today as Jerome, to revise the current Latin versions of the Bible. The next year this scholar gave the pope his first installment, the four Gospels. Jerome indicated that he had checked the Old Latin against the Greek. In the Old Testament he used the Septuagint but finally decided to translate the Hebrew original. To do this he secured the aid of Jewish rabbis.

Angry critics assailed Jerome because he made many changes in the Old Latin. Augustine was afraid Jerome was calling in doubt the divine inspiration of the Septuagint. The superior worth of the new revision was finally recognized, so it came to be called the Vulgate, or "common" version. Eventually, at the Council of Trent in 1545, the Roman Catholic Church identified the Vulgate as the official Latin text of the church. Over the years it has undergone several revisions. The second edition of *Nova Vulgata*, published in 1986, was authorized for use in current church liturgy.

Syriac Versions

Syriac is a Semitic language. Used in western Mesopotamia, it was closely related to the Aramaic dialect used in Palestine at the time of Christ.

a. Old Syriac. Like the Old Latin, the Old Syriac version rose in the second century. About the same time, around A.D. 170, Tatian produced his famous Diatessaron, a harmony of the Gospels in one continuous narrative. This is one of the proofs that our four Gospels, and no others, were accepted at that time, since only material from the four Gospels is used.

b. The Peshitta. Just as the Old Latin had been corrupted by many hands, so had the Old Syriac. So about the end of the fourth or beginning of the fifth century, a Peshitta ("simple") version was made. It became

the popular version for the Syriac churches, as the Vulgate did for the Latin.

During the early centuries many other versions were made. But we pass over all these to come immediately to what concerns us most, the translations into the English language.

English Versions

a. Early Beginnings. In his Ecclesiastical History

the Venerable Bede tells how the early English poet Caedmon (died 680) was a herdsman at the monastery of Whitby. One night in a dream he saw a man who told him to sing a song of the creation. In the morning he astonished everyone with his poetic gift. Brought into the monastery, Caedmon was told stories from the Bible and proceeded to turn them into Anglo-Saxon verse. He is said to have sung all the history of Genesis, the story of the Exodus, as well as the great truths of the New Testament. Some think only his original hymn of creation survives with certainty today. Before the death of Bede in 735, the four Gospels all appeared in Anglo-Saxon. Bede himself is credited with having translated the Gospel of John. Alfred, king of Wessex (848-901), was interested in the Bible and saw to it that a new translation of Psalms was made. Several other versions of parts of the Bible appeared in the following centuries.

b. Wycliffe's Bible (1382). John Wycliffe translated the first complete Bible into English. His translation was made from the Latin Vulgate, though, not the original Hebrew and Greek. Wycliffe's concern was to give the laity of his day a Bible they could read, as a part of the effort to reform the Church. In fact, he is called the "morning star of the Reformation." His English Bible did much to prepare the way for that movement in Britain. To get the Bible to the common people, Wycliffe organized the "Poor Priests," or Lollards, who went everywhere teaching the Bible and delivering it to the laypeo-

ple. Nearly two hundred copies of Wycliffe's Bible, or revisions of it, are still found in various libraries and museums. And this in spite of the fact that they were very expensive, being copied by hand, and that the authorities had passed a ruling that anyone who read the Scriptures in English "should forfeit land, catel, life, and goods from their heyres forever."[2]

John Wycliffe, a graduate of Oxford, became master of Balliol College. He was considered the most able theologian on the faculty. Yet his translation of the Bible was not well received by scholars and religious authorities of the time. Many considered it a threat to the Church.

In 1411 Archbishop Arundel wrote to the pope,

> This pestilent and wretched John Wyclif[fe], of cursed memory, that son of the old serpent . . . endeavoured by every means to attack the very faith and sacred doctrine of Holy Church, devising—to fill up the measure of his malice—the expedient of a new translation of the Scriptures into the mother tongue.[3]

Another contemporary with equal venom expressed his feelings as follows:

> This Master John Wyclif[fe] translated from Latin into English—the Angle not the angel speech—the Gospel that Christ gave to the clergy and doctors of the Church . . . so that by his means it has become vulgar and more open to laymen and women who can read than it usually is to quite learned clergy of good intelligence. And so the pearl of the Gospel is scattered abroad and trodden underfoot by swine.[4]

Wycliffe died in 1384, soon after finishing the translation. In 1428 his bones were disinterred and burned, and the ashes scattered on the river. Someone observed that as the waters of the river Swift carried these ashes onward to the Avon and Severn, and the Severn to the sea, so his influence spread far and wide.

c. Tyndale's New Testament (1526). Around 1456 the first book ever printed in Europe on movable type came off the press. It was the famous Gutenberg Bible, named after its printer, and was a copy of the Latin Vulgate. It was not until seventy years later that the first printed English New Testament appeared, translated by Tyndale.

William Tyndale received his M.A. at Oxford and went to Cambridge, where Erasmus had arrived in 1511 to teach Greek. When he left he soon became known as a keen debater. One day a learned man said to him, "We were better be without God's law than the Pope's." Tyndale's famous reply was "If God spare my lyfe, ere many yeares I wyl cause a boye that dryveth the plough shall know more of the scripture than thou doest."[5] This promise was fulfilled.

Tyndale wrote he "perceaved by experyence how that it was impossible to stablysh the laye people in any truth excepte the scripture were playnly layde before their eyes in their mother tonge," and added, "which thynge onlye moved me to translate the New Testament."[6]

He went to London, hoping to get support from the bishop there. Turned down by the bishop, he found a home with a prosperous merchant, Monmouth. For sheltering the "heretic," this businessman was later arrested and thrown into the Tower of London.

Frustrated in purpose, Tyndale wrote, "In London I abode almoste an yere . . . and understode at the laste not only that there was no rowme in my lorde of londons palace to translate the new testament, but also that there was no place to do it in al englonde."[7] So he left England. After a visit with Luther at Wittenberg and the receipt of funds from Monmouth, he hurried to Cologne in 1525. There he began printing his translation of the New Testament.

Difficulties dogged his steps. Cochlaeus, an enemy of the Reformation, invited some printers to his home. He plied them with wine until they talked too freely, and learned from them that 3,000 English copies of "The Lutheran New Testament" were right then on the press, being prepared for shipment to England. He obtained an injunction against the project. Tyndale and his assistant took a boat up the Rhine to Worms, carrying with them the sheets already printed. Here the printing was resumed. "The first complete printed New Testament in English appeared towards the end of February 1526, and copies were beginning to reach England about a month later."[8]

The reaction in England was twofold. As the copies of the New Testament were smuggled in, wrapped in merchandise, the people bought them eagerly. The ecclesiastical authorities became violent in their opposition. The bishop of

London said he could find 2,000 errors in Tyndale's New Testament and ordered all copies to be burned. By "errors" he actually meant changes from the Latin Vulgate. The archbishop raised funds with which to buy and burn them publicly. Cochlaeus, the old foe, made this classic speech:

> The New Testament translated into the vulgar [common] tongue is in truth the food of death, the fuel of sin, the veil of malice, the pretext of false liberty, the protection of disobedience, the corruption of discipline, the depravity of morals, the termination of concord, the death of honesty, the well-spring of vices, the disease of virtues, the instigation of rebellion, the milk of pride, the nourishment of contempt, the death of peace, the destruction of charity, the enemy of unity, the murderer of truth.[9]

It was a serious crime to translate the Word of God into the language of the common people!

Because of the strong opposition only three fragments now remain of the 18,000 copies printed between 1526 and 1528. The value of Tyndale's New Testament cannot be overestimated. It was made from the original Greek, not the Vulgate. Tyndale was a real scholar. In addition to Greek, he spoke Latin, Hebrew, French, Spanish, Italian, and German. His New Testament had a profound influence on subsequent translations. Herbert Gordon May writes,

> It has been estimated that one third of the King James Version of the New Testament is worded as Tyndale had it, and that even in the remaining two thirds the general literary structure set by Tyndale has been retained. Some scholars have said that ninety percent of Tyndale is reproduced in the King James Version of the New Testament.[10]

After finishing his New Testament translation, Tyndale started translating the Old Testament from the original Hebrew. In

1530 he published the Pentateuch. Twice (1534 and 1535) he revised his translation of the New Testament, seeking to make it as nearly perfect as possible. Apparently he also translated from Joshua to Chronicles, though this was not published until after his death.

In May 1535 a supposed friend had Tyndale treacherously arrested in Antwerp, Belgium, where he was living in exile from England. He was imprisoned for over a year. While in prison he wrote a letter in Latin to the governor of the castle where he was held. It bears a striking resemblance to Paul's words written from prison in Rome (2 Timothy 4:9-21). We quote a part of the English translation:

> Wherefore I beg . . . that if I am to remain here through the winter, you will request the commissary to have the kindness to send me, from the goods of mine which he has, a warmer cap; for I suffer greatly from cold in the head, and am much afflicted by a perpetual catarrh, which is much increased in this cell; a warmer coat also, for this which I have is very thin. . . . My overcoat is worn out; my shirts are also worn out. . . . And I ask to be allowed to have a lamp in the evening; it is indeed wearisome sitting alone in the dark. But most of all I beg . . . to have the Hebrew Bible, Hebrew grammar, and Hebrew dictionary, that I may pass the time in that study.[11]

There is no indication this request was granted. In 1536 Tyndale was condemned for heresy, strangled, and burned at the stake. His famous last words were "Lord, open the King of England's eyes." He did not have the satisfaction of knowing that some months before, King Henry VIII had given his permission for the circulation in England of the Coverdale Bible, which incorporated most of Tyndale's work.

d. Coverdale's Bible (1535). The first complete printed English Bible was issued by Myles Coverdale in 1535. Educated at Cambridge, he had to live on the European continent while he worked on his translation from 1528 to 1534. He was not an original scholar like Tyndale. Fortunately, his New Testament is only a revision of Tyndale's. He leaned heavily on the latter's translation of the Pentateuch. Coverdale must be given credit for his efforts to make the whole Bible available in English. To this task he devoted much of his adult life.

e. The Matthew Bible (1537). This Bible, which was printed on the Continent under the pen name of Thomas Matthew, was largely a revision of Tyndale's material. It was actually the work of John Rogers, to whom Tyndale turned over his translations when he was imprisoned. Rogers himself was later burned at the stake.

f. The Great Bible (1539). Thomas Cromwell asked Coverdale to prepare another version, based on the Matthew Bible. The measure of Coverdale's devotion to the Word of God is shown by the fact he was willing to see his own Bible set aside in order to gain wider circulation for a new version.

The printing began in Paris, where better presses and paper were available. In spite of the fact the French king licensed the project, the Inquisition stopped the printing, attempting to seize pages already completed. The type, presses, and workmen were finally moved to London, where work was finished.

The final product was called the Great Bible because of its size. The pages measured sixteen-and-a-half by eleven inches. This Bible became the first authorized English version. The 1540 edition had on the title page "This is the Byble apoynted to the use of the churches." The next year the king issued a proclamation "for the Byble of the largest and greatest volume to be had in every church."

Copies of the Great Bible were placed in the churches, chained to a lectern so that they would not be stolen. People gathered eagerly around these to hear the Word of God read aloud. This activity even went on during the sermon, much to the annoyance of the parsons! The enthusiastic response of the people is shown in the fact that seven printings of this Bible were made within three years.

In the same year (1539) the Taverner Bible appeared. Taverner was a layman, a graduate of Oxford with an excellent knowledge of Greek. While he reprinted the Old Testament of the Matthew Bible with little change, he made many revisions in the New Testament.

The deſcription of the holie land and of the places mencioned in the foure Euangeliſtes.

g. *The Geneva Bible (1560)*. The period between 1539 and 1560 was hectic for the new English Bibles and their promoters. Under heavy Roman Catholic pressure, King Henry VIII reversed his tolerant attitude. In 1543 an act of Parliament forbade using all translations bearing the name of Tyndale. No working man or woman was to read the Bible, on pain of imprisonment.

The next king, Edward VI, was a strong Protestant and sought to restore the Bible to the common people. In this Archbishop Cranmer supported him. Unfortunately, Edward's reign was short (1547 to 1553). He was succeeded by Queen Mary, a fanatical Roman Catholic. During her violent reign of five years no fewer than three hundred Protestant reformers were put to death, including Cranmer and Rogers.

Coverdale escaped to the Continent and joined the band of vigorous Protestants at Geneva. There a group of scholars worked "night and day for two and a half years" to produce the Geneva Bible. It was the first complete English Bible to be divided into verses. It also contained many helpful notes for the common reader. With good reason it became the people's book in England and Scotland. In fact, it was the first Bible to be published in Scotland. The Scottish Parliament passed an act that every home that could afford it should possess a copy of the Bible.

The Geneva version was the Bible of John Bunyan and William Shakespeare. It was also the Bible of the Pilgrim Fathers. It is sometimes called the "Breeches Bible" because it translated Genesis 3:7—"They sewed fig leaves together and made themselves breeches."

As in Coverdale's Bible, the Apocrypha was placed between the Old and New Testament as an appendix. But the Geneva reformers were careful to state that these books were not "to be read and expounded publicly in the Church, neither yet served to prove any point of Christian religion."

h. The Bishops' Bible (1568). For some years there were two main Bibles in England. The Geneva was the Bible of the people, and the Great Bible was for the pulpits in the churches. Finally Archbishop Parker ordered a revision of the Great Bible, hoping it would take the place of both versions. Because many of the scholars who did the work of revising were bishops, it was called the Bishops' Bible.

Unfortunately, the bishops loved their Latin. So for "love" in 1 Corinthians 13 in the earlier versions, they substituted "charity," from the Latin Vulgate *caritas.* This sad mistake was carried over into the King James Version, which was a revision of the Bishops' Bible.

i. The Douay-Rheims Version (1609-10). The Roman Catholic leaders were disturbed by the fact Protestants were becoming very familiar with the Bible in their mother tongue. So—unwillingly, as they themselves stated—they decided to put out an English version of their own. The New Testament was completed in 1582 at Rheims, France. The Old Testament was published, 1609-10, at Douay, in Flanders. As expected, both were translated from the Latin Vulgate, the official Catholic Bible.

The translation is wooden and often obscure. Latinisms abound. For instance, it speaks of "supersubstantial" bread and says of one person that he "exinanited himself." One particularly objectionable feature is the use of "do penance" for "repent."

j. The King James Version (1611). When James VI of Scotland became James I of England (following the death of Queen Elizabeth I in 1603), he called the churchmen together for a conference at Hampton Court (1604). There John Reynolds, a prominent Puritan leader and president of Corpus Christi College, Oxford, proposed this resolution: "That a translation be made of the whole Bible, as consonant as can be to the original Hebrew and Greek; and this to be set out and printed, without any marginal notes, and only to be used in all Churches of England in time of divine service."

The bishop of London (later Archbishop of Canterbury) objected, saying, "If every man's humour were followed, there would be no end of translating." Undaunted, King James heartily approved the resolution and actively promoted the work. By July 1604 he had "appointed certain learned men to the number of four and fifty for the translating of the Bible." Only forty-seven names are on the list of those who actually worked on the translation. They were divided into six panels, with three panels for the Old Testament, two for the New Testament, and one for the Apocrypha. Two groups met at Oxford, two at Cambridge, and two at Westminster.

Fifteen ground rules were set up by the translators. The first read, "The Bishops' Bible to be followed, and as little altered as the truth of the original will permit." It is clear this was to be a revision of the Bishops' Bible. Interestingly, it was specified that use should be made of the Tyndale, Matthew, Coverdale, or Great Bible when any of these agreed more closely with the original text than did the Bishops' Bible.

The rules further called for close cooperation between members of each group. When the work was finished, two members from each of the three centers met as a committee to go over the final translation before it was printed. Thus the effort was made to assure a job well done. The actual work of translation took four years (1607 to 1611).

It is often assumed that the King James Version, as it is called, has come down to us exactly in its original form. This is not true. The fact is that the original edition of the King James Version would make difficult reading for the average reader. In 1613, only two years after it was first published, over three hundred variations were introduced. Another revision came out in 1629 and still another in 1638. It was the revision made at Oxford in 1769 that modernized its spelling so it can be read with some ease today. This is essentially the version we now have.

There was one rule given the original translators they failed to follow, and, their mistake was never corrected. They were told to use the commonly known form of proper names. The King James Version has "Isaiah" in the Old Testament and "Esaias" in the New; "Jeremiah" and "Jeremias," "Elijah" and "Elias," and so forth.

The strength of the King James Version was its beautiful Elizabethan English prose. For this reason it became the most widely used English Bible for three centuries. William Lyons Phelps, famous teacher of literature at Yale University, once said Shakespeare and the King James Version standardized the English language.

Often the King James Version is referred to as "The Authorized Version" (AV). This is incorrect. The Great Bible of 1539 and the Bishops' Bible of 1560 were both authorized versions. The King James Version of 1611 carries on the title page "Appointed to be read in the churches." But there is no record of any official action ever taken to authorize this.

In view of the opposition to some recent versions, it is interesting to note the King James Version suffered similarly at first. Hugh Broughton, one of the greatest Greek and Hebrew scholars of his day, wrote,

> The late Bible . . . was sent to me to censure: which bred in me a sadness that will grieve me while I breathe, it is so ill done. Tell His Majesty that I had rather be rent in pieces with wild horses, than any such translation by my consent should be urged upon poor churches . . . The new edition crosseth me. I require it to be burnt.[12]

Some critics of the King James Version went further in their denunciations. They accused the translators of blasphemy and called them "damnable corruptors" of God's Word.[13]

The Pilgrims who came to the New World in 1620 refused to have anything to do with the King James Version. They preferred the Geneva Bible and continued to use it. In fact, it was not until 1777 that the New Testament of the King James Version was published in America. The complete Bible finally came out in 1782.

Gradually the King James Version supplanted the Geneva Bible in the new nation of the United States. After some years it became the dominant Bible, as it was in England.

Perhaps some reader has wondered why most people, when repeating the Lord's Prayer, say, "And forgive us our trespasses, as we forgive those who trespass against us." This often became awkward in public worship when some people use the shorter form found in our King James Version, "And forgive us our debts, as we forgive our debtors" (Matthew 6:12). Where did the other come from?

The answer is that in the Book of Common Prayer of the Church of England the Scripture quotations were taken from the Coverdale Bible and were never revised to conform to the King James Version.

It is unfortunate that some of our present copies of the King James Version carry in the front of them the dedication to King James. It is full of false flattery and entirely worthless today. The original Preface, "The Translators to the Readers," is omitted. In this the scholars expressed their dismay at the prevailing attitude of people toward a new translation of the Bible. They wrote,

Zeal to promote the common good, whether it be by devising anything ourselves, or revising that which hath been laboured by others, deserveth certainly much respect and esteem, but yet findeth but cold entertainment in the world. It is welcomed with suspicion instead of love, and with emulation instead of thanks: and if there be any hole left for cavil to enter, (and cavil, if it do not find a hole, will make one) is sure to be misconstrued, and in danger to be condemned. This will easily be granted by as many as know history, or have any experience. For, was there ever anything projected, that savoured any way of newness of renewing, but the same endured many a storm of gainsaying, or opposition?

It is obvious people of the seventeenth century took the same attitude as some people of the twentieth and twenty-first centuries toward new translations of the Bible!

In many ways the King James translators did a magnificent job. They gave the Bible a poetic prose that has sung its way across four centuries. There is a rhythmic beauty in the language of the King James Version that will always afford pleasure to many readers.

This should not blind us to an important fact underscored by C. S. Lewis in his little book *The Literary Impact of the Authorized Version.* He says, "Those who read the Bible as literature do not read the Bible."[14] He declares that the Bible is "not merely a sacred book but a book so remorselessly and continuously sacred that it does not invite, it excludes or repels the merely aesthetic approach."[15] To appreciate these statements one must remember that C. S. Lewis was not a preacher or a theologian but a famous teacher of English literature at Oxford and Cambridge universities.

The Bible was not written to entertain but to redeem. Consequently, we should seek to have the Scriptures in a translation that conveys exactly and accurately as possible what the original language says.

Questions

1. What is the Septuagint, and what place did it have in the Early Church?

2. What is the Vulgate, and what place has it filled in history?

3. What was the first English Bible, and from what was it translated?

4. Who made the first printed English New Testament, and how did his work influence the King James Version?

5. What was the Bible of the Puritans and Pilgrims?

6. When was the King James Version made, and what was the secret of its final popularity?

Its Five Propagation

O for a thousand tongues to sing
My great Redeemer's praise,
The glories of my God and King,
The triumphs of His grace!
My gracious Master and my God,
Assist me to proclaim,
To spread thro' all the earth abroad,
The honors of Thy name.

So wrote Charles Wesley over two centuries ago. Little did he dream within that period of time the Bible would be translated into over a thousand tongues, spreading throughout the world.

Charles Wesley died in 1788, and his more famous brother, John, in 1791. The next year, 1792, marks the beginning of the great modern era of world missions. More was done to evangelize the world in the next one hundred fifty years than had been done in the previous 1,500 years.

William Carey was a Baptist preacher in England. So poor was his congregation that he had to support his family by making shoes. His heart was burdened for the millions of people in Asia and Africa who had never heard the gospel. Above his cobbler's bench he hung a map of the world. With John Wesley he could say, "The world is my parish." In spite of the pressure of pastoral duties and working for a living, Carey mastered Latin, Greek, and Hebrew. One day he preached a sermon on "Expect great things from God; attempt great things for God." As a result, the first Baptist missionary society was founded in 1792. The next year William Carey and his family sailed for India, accompanied by John Thomas, who had lived in Bengal.

Soon after they arrived, all their property was lost in the Hooghly River. Only his rugged faith in God kept William Carey going. He took a job in an indigo factory, because funds from the home society had failed to come. This new employment gave him close contact with the nationals. It was invaluable in helping him learn their language. For five years he studied the Bengali and Sanskrit languages.

Finally, at Serampore, he translated the New Testament into Bengali and published it in 1801. For thirty years Carey taught Bengali, Marathi, and Sanskrit. This brought him into contact with leading Indian intellectuals. With their help he was able to translate the Scriptures into all the principal languages of northern Hindustan. He used his salary to establish a press on which these were printed.

The total production of William Carey and his helpers is staggering. He is credited with the translation of the whole Bible into nine languages, the New Testament into twenty-seven more, and smaller portions of Scripture into several others.

> The whole number of languages is stated at forty, and we are probably below the truth when we state that the Serampore press, under the auspices chiefly of Dr. Carey, was honored to be the instrument, in about thirty years, of rendering the Word of God accessible to three hundred millions of human beings, or nearly one third of the population of the world.[1]

All humanity is deeply indebted to such individuals of vision and courage as William Carey. One is tempted to wonder what the history of the nineteenth and twentieth centuries would have been if God had a hundred Careys to carry on the work of His kingdom.

A few statistics help put in bold relief what we have said thus far. Eric N. North, in his introductory essay "And Now—in a Thousand Tongues," writes, "It is estimated on the eve of the invention of printing only thirty-three languages—twenty-two European, seven Asian, four African—had any part of the Bible translated."[2] More surprising is the statement "But even by 1800 only seventy-one languages and dialects had seen some printed portion of the Bible—fifty in Europe, thirteen in Asia, four in Africa, three in the Americas (Massachusetts, Mohawk, and Arawak), and one in Oceania."[3]

Then the picture changed radically. At last the Holy Spirit found a few through whom He could work. North says,

> The next thirty years saw an amazing expansion. Eighty-six languages received some part of the Bible—more than in all the 1800 years before! And sixty-six of these were languages outside of Europe! The missionary movement, with

its roots watered and fertilized by the Evangelical Revival of the eighteenth century, bore this sudden burst of bloom.[4]

One result was the British and Foreign Bible Society, founded in 1804, and the American Bible Society, founded in 1816. Throughout the nineteenth and twentieth centuries over one hundred Bible societies were founded with the main purpose of making the Bible available to all people. In 1946 they formed a cooperative organization called the United Bible Society, joining forces seeking to spread the Bible around the world in as many languages as possible.

By 1938 the translations of Scripture passed the 1,000 mark. Of these, one hundred seventy-three were in Europe, two hundred twelve in Asia, three hundred forty-five in Africa, eighty-nine in the Americas, and one hundred eighty-nine in Oceania. By the end of the twentieth century the 2,000 mark had been attained. The total figure at the beginning of the twenty-first century is over 2,400 languages into which the Bible, in whole or in part, has been translated. The Wycliffe Bible Translators and the United Bible Societies have been most active in this.

We shall take a glimpse at the spread of Bible translations in different world areas. Only a few high points can be noted.

Europe

It has been said Martin Luther's most important and lasting contribution to the Protestant Reformation was not his preaching or teaching but rather his translation of the Bible into the German of his day. There was a medieval German version available, but it was made from the Latin Vulgate and poorly done. Luther used the Greek text in his lectures on Romans in 1515-16 and the Hebrew in his commentary on Hebrews in 1517-18. He was well prepared for his work of translating the Bible from the original.

The story of his project is fascinating. As Luther returned from the Diet of Worms (1521), where he made his famous "Here I stand" speech, friends were fearful for his life. So they spirited him away to the castle of Wartburg. There he spent the winter in safe hiding.

In December he made a hurried, secret trip to Wittenberg. There his friend Philip Melancthon advised him to make a translation of the New Testament. When he again visited Wittenberg on March 6, 1522, he already had the first draft completed—in two and a half months! With Melancthon's help he revised it, and it was published in September 1522. Luther spent twelve more years, with interruptions due to illness and other duties, translating the Old Testament. Finally his entire German Bible was published in 1534 and became a major bulwark of the Reformation.

Fig. 322. — Martin Luther, facsimile réduit d'un portrait de Lucas de Cranach (1520), placé en tête d'un sermon que Luther prononça contre l'autorité de l'Église romaine, en quittant non livré de moins augustin: Wittenberg, 1520, in-4°. — Le distiques latin célèbre ainsi l'artiste et le modèle : « Si Luther laisse de son génie des traces impérissables, Lucas (Cranach) fixe à tout jamais les traits que la mort efface. »

religieux qui tenait l'Europe attentive et tremblante, apparaissent bien moins dans les gros livres, publiés depuis par la controverse savante, que dans ces feuilles éparses et jetées au vent, criées par les rues, chantées aux carrefours

Of the literary significance of this translation Hans Volz says,

> Luther's Bible was a literary event of the first magnitude, for it is the first work of art in German prose. . . . The Bible first became a real part of the literary heritage of the German people with Luther. . . . In the history of the language his version is also a factor whose significance cannot be overestimated in the development of the vocabulary of modern literary German.[5]

The average North American has no idea how many languages are spoken in Europe, even today. While the many different

Indo-European languages (Germanic, Romance, Slavic and others) are most predominant, there are literally dozens of other minority languages spoken. By 2007 some of the Scriptures were translated into no fewer than two hundred twelve languages of that continent.

At least everybody in the British Isles uses English. Well, not quite. Many people in Wales cling to their native Welsh, as became apparent when Prince Charles was inaugurated as the Prince of Wales. The earliest Welsh Bible appeared over four hundred years ago, in 1588. The New Testament was translated into Irish by the middle of the fourteenth century. During the twentieth century there was a revival of the old Gaelic language in Eire (Republic of Ireland). The Gaelic of the Scottish Highlands is closely related to the Gaelic of Ireland. The Scots had their own New Testament as early as 1767.

Herein lies an interesting tale. The Scottish Society for the Propagation of the Gospel opposed the use of the Scriptures in Gaelic. The famous Samuel Johnson urged "the holy books" should be given to the people in their own language. He wrote, "To omit for a year, or for a day, the most efficacious method of advancing Christianity . . . is a crime." It took the great dictionary-maker to tell religious leaders what their duty was!

The large island of Iceland had the entire Bible in the Scandinavian language by 1584, thanks to King Frederick II of Denmark. He ordered every church to have a copy. The bishop of the island arranged for the poorest people to receive free copies. The Iceland Bible Society was founded in 1815 and reported three years later that every family had either a Bible or a New Testament. Scriptures were read with diligence during the long winter evenings.

Parts of the New Testament were translated into at least three *Romani* dialects for the gypsies of central Europe. A gypsy who made one translation became a Bible Society book salesman and then an evangelist. One remarkable experience took place at the grave of a fellow gypsy. After the Roman Catholic priest conducted the service in unintelligible Latin, the book salesman stepped up and read the story of Lazarus ("I Am the Resurrection and the Life") in the familiar language of the people.

The Bible spread to all of Europe and to all classes of people. Thousands of copies were carried behind the infamous "iron curtain" during the twentieth century. *God's Smuggler,* by "Brother Andrew," is a thrilling story of how Scriptures were carried, at great risk of life, into all the formerly Communist countries of Eastern Europe.

Asia

It was in Asia that much of the Bible was written. Here many of the earliest translations were made. Among them were the Old Syriac (second century) and the Armenian (fifth century), as well as the earlier Aramaic and Samaritan Targums.

It is an apparent tragedy that Scriptures were not translated into Arabic until a century after Mohammed's death. Had Mohammed possessed the New Testament in his own language, how different might have been the religious history of Africa and Asia for the past fourteen centuries!

The power of the printed word is one of the important factors in history. R. Kilgour writes,

The Bible has been described as the unfettered missionary. It reaches where the Christian preacher is forbidden to enter. It knows no boundaries of closed lands. Human agents may be excluded, but the printed page finds its way in. Anti-Christian Governments may promulgate laws against it, may even confiscate existing copies; but the history of Christianity abundantly proves that nothing can wholly eradicate its message. In a most marvelous manner the Word of God liveth and abideth forever.[6]

This truth is especially exemplified in the Himalayan area of central Asia. For centuries the four countries of Afghanistan, Tibet, Nepal, and Bhutan remained tightly closed against any Christian preachers. At least parts of the Bible have been translated into all the main tribal languages of these nations.

Nepal is one case in point. William Carey and his colleagues translated the New Testament into at least four dialects of Nepal. It was not until 1914 that the whole Bible became available in Nepalese. Thousands of copies of Scripture found their way across the border into this forbidden land. Resulting from this, Christian missionaries are now at work in Nepal. Even in Tibet, "the roof of the world," the Bible is present in the language of the people.

It was in Nepal that Sadhu Sundar Singh lost his life, seeking to carry the gospel to these people. He already had experienced a great ministry in India. Led to Christ himself by reading the New Testament, he was always sharing it with the Hindus.

One day on a train he gave a copy of John's Gospel to another traveler. The man read a little from it, then tore it up, throwing the pieces out the window.

Two years later Sadhu Sundar Singh learned that a seeker after truth found those torn scraps of paper. On one fragment were the words "the Bread of Life." Hungering to know what this meant, he purchased a New Testament, was converted, and became a preacher of the gospel. Said Singh, "Really the torn pieces of St. John's Gospel proved to be a piece of the living Bread—the Bread of life."

The story of William Carey's translations of the Scriptures in India has been told, though briefly. One incident might be added. When a Baptist mission opened in Dacca in 1818, several villages were found in which the peasants called themselves "Satyagurus" (religious teachers). They showed the missionaries a much-worn book, kept carefully in a wooden box. It was a copy of Carey's first Bengali New Testament, issued in 1801. Though the villagers did not know from where it came, they found in it a new faith.

One area in which the Church of the Nazarene in India operates is a Marathi-speaking area. The New Testament was translated into this language in 1811 and the whole Bible eight years later. This was another product of Carey's group at Serampore. Since then the Marathi Christians themselves have taken an active part in revising the translation for use today.

The Syrian Church of Malabar in southern India was conducting its services in Syriac, a foreign language, when a Protestant missionary arrived. The people spoke Malayalam, as they do today. The missionary made available a translation of the Gospels in their mother tongue.

The story of the Bible translation work done by Robert Morrison, the first Protestant missionary to China, is not as startling as that of William Carey in India. It is, however, a noble tale in its own right.

Morrison was only ten years old when Carey launched his missionary enterprise in 1792. After elementary instruction in the "three R's" (reading, writing, and 'rithmetic), he was apprenticed at a very early age to his father, who made shoe lasts. His widow tells of his eagerness to study:

> For the purpose of securing a greater portion of quiet retirement, he had his bed removed to his workshop, where he would often pursue his studies until one or two in the morning. Even when at work, his Bible or some other book was placed open before him, that he might acquire knowledge

or cherish the holy aspirations of spiritual devotion while his hands were busily occupied in the labors of life.[7]

At nineteen years of age Morrison was ready to begin his study of Hebrew, Latin, and theology. It was not long until he felt a missionary concern. He offered himself to the London Missionary Society. While at its mission school he studied Chinese with a resident of the town from China. In 1807 he went to that distant land. Morrison labored for seven years before winning his first Chinese convert.

In the meantime Morrison was not idle. By 1814 his Chinese translation of the New Testament was ready for the press. Another missionary arrived in 1813 and presumably helped Morrison finish the New Testament. At any rate, they worked together on the Old Testament translation and completed it in 1819.

In India over two hundred languages and approximately eight hundred dialects are spoken. While the situation in China is much better, there are various dialects into which the Scriptures must yet be translated.

The story of one of these translations serves to illustrate the dedication of translators to their task. It also shows the power of the Word.

On the Malabar coast of India a scholarly black Jew translated the New Testament into Hebrew for the purpose of refuting Christianity. More than a century later, a Jewish man in Lithuania came across a Hebrew New Testament based on this translation. He read it and was converted. Emigrating to New York, he entered General Theological Seminary. A brilliant linguist, he was offered a professorship. He declined it, saying he was called to go to China to translate the Bible. Since the New Testament had already been published in northern Mandarin, the missionary, Samuel Schereschewsky, tackled the Old Testament, finishing it in four years.

A sun stroke brought on a spinal disease that left him an invalid the rest of his life. All he could use was one finger of each hand. Lifted into his chair each morning, he worked twenty-five years without quitting. With his two good fingers he tapped out his translation in Roman letters on a typewriter, and then his Chinese colleagues wrote it in Chinese characters. In this way he completed the Old Testament in another dialect, which already had the New Testament. And so the whole Bible was at last available to millions of people in their own tongue.

Africa

As a continent, Africa came of age later than other global areas. As would be expected, Bible translation was slow here. This led the way, however, in the development of literature. Kilgour writes,

> Most African languages were reduced to writing in the first instance with the express purpose of being the vehicle of teaching God's Word. Some piece of Scripture is usually the earliest specimen of printing in these tongues.[8]

Once work began, it moved forward rapidly. When the British and Foreign Bible Society was organized in 1804, only four African languages had any Scriptures in them. In 1876 this number was over fifty. By 1938 it was about three hundred fifty. By the beginning of the twenty-first century this number had doubled.

There are still many African tongues into which no part of the Bible has been translated. One authority lists the names of three hundred sixty-six Bantu dialects, and this is just one of five main families of African speech.

The almost total eclipse of the Christian Church in North Africa is an unparalleled tragedy in history. In the second through fourth centuries, Carthage was one of the great centers of Christianity. Even the temple of Venus in that city was turned into a Christian church. Among the great church fathers, Tertullian, Cyprian, and Augustine were North Africans. The Muslim conquest of the seventh century left hardly a vestige of the Christian faith in this area where the gospel had been preached so eloquently.

Why? Kilgour suggests one reason that is worth considering. He says,

> The great warning from North Africa is that, alongside of preaching, there must be the Bible in the vernacular. Egypt, Syria, Armenia and Georgia prove that no Church which had the Scriptures in the speech of the common people has ever completely perished, and the task today is to repair the error which cost North Africa such a price.[9]

Samuel Zwemer, a leading authority on missions among Muslims, tells of the visit of a book salesman to Somaliland, in eastern Africa. Forty years later another man went there on the same errand. He found an old Arab who still had the Arabic Bible he bought from the previous book salesman. He still prayed the Lord's Prayer and, after forty years, had not forgotten the gos-

pel message. Examples may be given from every continent regarding the power of the written Word to save humanity by the living Word.

Henry M. Stanley is well known for his trip into Africa's jungles to find David Livingstone. One of the dramatic moments of history is the final meeting of the two men and Livingstone's refusal to return to civilization. The cry of Africa's heart held his heart in a viselike grip. He could not leave.

Not commonly known is the fact that Stanley, with the help of an African boy and the king's scribe, was the first to translate a few verses of the Bible (the Ten Commandments) into the native language of Uganda. In answer to his plea, the Church Missionary Society sent an emissary.

Alexander Mackay, a brilliant young Scottish engineer, reduced Uganda's language to writing in 1880. With his own hands he cut out wooden type and printed portions of his new translation of Scripture. In spite of persecution that caused the murder of Bishop Hannington in October 1885, the very next month Mackay printed three hundred fifty copies of the first sheets of Matthew. The work continued until the entire Bible was finished in 1896, six years after his death. In Uganda the term "reader" came to mean "Christian."

One of the epics of missionary lore is the story of Madagascar. Roman Catholics entered the island off the east coast of Africa with little success. When Protestant missionaries came in 1818, they used an entirely different approach. The first thing they did was translate God's Word into Malagasy, completing the entire Bible in ten years.

In 1835, when church membership had reached about 200, the "killing times" began. The queen forbade anybody to possess Christian Scriptures on pain of death. Many who refused to give them up were tortured and killed.

Before the missionaries were expelled, they buried in the ground seventy copies of the Bible and stored Scripture portions in other places—to be read by the persecuted Christians. Kilgour tells the result:

> When the reign of terror ended after a quarter of a century, the little Church had increased tenfold, having been

nourished, sustained, comforted and strengthened by one spiritual teacher, counselor, friend and guide in this world and to the next, the Word of God which is able to make men wise unto Salvation.[10]

Now the Christian Church of Madagascar includes hundreds of thousands and has sent missionaries to other areas.

At the beginning of the twentieth century exciting reports were coming out of Africa about "Prophet Harris." Dressed in white robe and turban, William Wade Harris carried a rough wooden cross in his right hand and an English Bible in his left. In each town he entered he placed the open Bible in the center of the crowd and denounced evil and idolatry. As a result of his preaching, British missionaries gathered many converts into churches and instructed them in Christianity. Investigation revealed Harris was born and brought up in a Liberian village where a pioneer missionary translated the Scriptures into his mother tongue. This influence led him to become the flaming evangelist of West Africa.

In the Congo missionaries worked for years to translate the Bible into a combined dialect, completing it in 1930. The effect of this on the Mongo tribe was tellingly illustrated within a short time. In 1894, at the funeral of a chief, forty young men were beheaded and their corpses buried with him. Many more were killed to provide for the feast that followed. Forty years later, in 1934, a Communion service was attended by some of the same people. Enemies who formerly met only to kill and eat human flesh now sat together at the Lord's table. Instead of being armed with spears and knives, they carried their Bibles.

South America

In his book *Adventures with the Bible in Brazil*, Frederick Glass tells how as a book salesman he was selling Scriptures in a town. A farmer came to him and told him that he had purchased a copy of the Bible years before. He said, "I want you to come to my village." There Glass found a group of eager worshipers. The farmer had called in his friends and neighbors and read the Word of God to them. Soon many of them had repented of their sins and were saved. Though they had never seen a white missionary or heard a Christian sermon, there were eleven converts who were ready for baptism. As a result, a new Christian village was formed.

The main language of Brazil is Portuguese. Spanish is used throughout most of the remainder of the continent, Central America, and Mexico. There are hundreds of Indian tribes whose people speak only their own native dialect. Consequently, the Wycliffe Translators are constantly at work, translating the Word of God into languages of the various tribes.

As an example, William Sedat, who translated the entire New Testament into Kekchi in Guatemala, gives John 14:1— "Let not your heart be troubled" (KJV) this way: "Don't shiver in your liver."

The Pacific Islands

Two Wesleyan missionaries landed in the Fiji Islands in 1835. By 1864 they had translated the entire Bible into the leading Polynesian dialect. That very year the "Crier of War" drum called the people together. This time it was not for a cannibal feast but to see the king, his family, and many warriors bow before the King of Kings. A month or two later the first Fiji edition of the Bible reached a neighboring island, and its king was converted. Twenty years later the murder stone, on which victim's heads had been dashed, was hollowed into a baptismal font.

A missionary named John Geddie settled on one of the islands of the New Hebrides in 1848. At once he set to work translating the Gospel of Mark. It was published in 1853. Ten years later the New Testament appeared, and in 1879 the entire Bible. The epitaph on his tombstone reads as follows:

WHEN HE CAME IN 1848
THERE WAS NOT A CHRISTIAN;
WHEN HE DIED IN 1872
THERE WAS NOT A HEATHEN.

John G. Paton worked on another New Hebrides island, Aniwa. He, too, was concerned to give islanders the Bible in their languages. The frustrating fact was that there were no words in their language remotely resembling the great Christian concepts of grace and faith. How could you tell people to believe on the Lord Jesus when there was no word for "believe"?

One day Paton was working in his hut on his new translation. A man came in. Weary with walking, he slumped down onto a chair. As he did so he said, "I'm leaning my whole weight on this chair." Eagerly the missionary asked him to repeat the phrase. In that edition of the New Testament "believe" is translated "lean your whole weight on"—a good definition for all Christians!

Stories could be multiplied about the effect of God's Word on people. The following is a final one.

The Maoris of New Zealand were especially fierce. The Bible was finally complete in their language in 1924.

At a Communion service a missionary noticed a Maori withdraw from the altar and go back to his seat. After a while he returned and partook.

This was the man's explanation. He found himself before the Communion table kneeling beside a man who had killed his father and drunk his blood. He had sworn to kill this man the first time he saw him. Here are the man's words:

So I went back to my seat. Then I saw in the spirit the upper sanctuary, and I seemed to hear a voice, "Hereby shall

all men know that ye are my disciples, if ye love one another." And I saw another sight, a Cross and a Man nailed on it, and I heard Him say, "Father, forgive them, for they know not what they do." Then I went back to the altar.[11]

These many stories remind us of the power of God's Word. While the Bible has been made available in thousands of languages, there is still much to be done. Of the nearly 7,000 languages spoken in the world, over 2,000 have no portion of the Bible translated. More than one hundred ninety million people speak these languages. Most of them live in Central Africa, southeast Asia, and the Pacific islands. The vision of Wycliffe Bible Translators still seeks fulfillment: "God's Word, accessible to all people in the language of their heart."

Questions

1. What man is considered the father of modern missions, and what contribution did he make to Bible translations?

2. What was the importance of Luther's translation of the Bible?

3. Why did the Church fail in North Africa?

4. What did Morrison do for the cause of missions in China?

5. What sacrifices did Alexander Mackay make in order to give the Bible to Uganda?

6. What effect has the Bible had in South America?

Its Six
Communication

It took 80 years for the King James Version (1611) to win complete acceptance in the English-speaking world. Luther A. Weigle writes, "It was denounced as theologically unsound and ecclesiastically biased, as truckling to the king and unduly deferring to his belief in witchcraft, as untrue to the Hebrew text and relying too much on the Septuagint."[1] The translators themselves recognize in their Preface that every new translation is apt to be "glouted upon by every evil eye" and "gored by every sharp tongue." The Puritans in the British Isles and the Pilgrims in America clung tenaciously to their beloved Geneva Bible and did not wish to give it up for this "newfangled" version.

Finally the King James Version became the dominant English Bible and held this position for over two centuries. This was largely because of its superior literary style and its Elizabethan prose. The English of the KJV is not the spoken or written language of our day. As a result, the modern era has produced an abundant crop of new English translations. During the last half of the twentieth century and the first decade of twenty-first, over fifty translations have been offered to readers.

Individual Translations

Translations by individuals began much earlier, even in the seventeenth century. In 1645 the Hebrew scholar John Lightfoot urged the House of Commons "to think of a review and survey of the translation of the Bible," that "the three nations [England, Ireland, Scotland] might come to understand the proper and

genuine study of the Scriptures by an exact, vigorous, and lively translation."[2] Several paraphrases of the New Testament appeared soon after this.

a. John Wesley's New Testament (1755). The eighteenth century produced several individual translations, of which the most significant was John Wesley's. In his preface, Wesley indicated the King James Version needed improvement in three areas: a better Greek text, better interpretation, and better English. So concerned was he about this that he devoted his best energies to the task. He felt this was an important factor in supporting and supplementing his preaching of scriptural salvation.

Wesley worked from the Greek New Testament, which had been his constant companion for many years. In line with his goal, he sought to establish the best Greek text available, making careful use of Bengel's *Gnomon*. This source was published in Germany in 1742, based on Bengel's critical apparatus of 1734. In this respect Wesley was far ahead of most preachers of his day. He realized Christian holiness demanded honest scholarship. He was sincere in his desire and worked hard to discover the best Greek text and translate it accurately and clearly.

A careful study of John Wesley's New Testament shows 12,000 changes from the King James Version, many of them examples of better English. In over 6,500 occurrences John Wesley's translation of the New Testament (1755) agreed with the *Revised Standard Version* (1946) against the King James Version (1611). In about four hundred thirty of these Wesley used a better Greek text than that on which the King James Version was based. This fact alone shows the biblical scholarship of this preacher who desired to communicate the Word of God accurately and effectively to his generation. Unfortunately, too few of his followers have followed his example.

During the nineteenth century individual translations were put out by such men as Noah Webster (1833), of dictionary fame, and Robert Young (1862), who compiled the *Analytical Concordance of the Bible*. The latter made a very literal rendering of the original Hebrew and Greek. Neither of these translations left any permanent effect.

As the twentieth century unfolded, many more individual translations appeared. Each attempted to render the Bible more readable. These included *The New Testament in Modern Speech,* by Richard Weymouth (1903); *The New Testament: A New Translation,* by James Moffat (1926); *An American Translation,* by Edgar J. Goodspeed (1939); *The Holy Bible: The Berke-*

ley Version in Modern English, by Gerrit Verkuyl (1959); and *The New Testament in the Language of Today,* by William Beck (1963). Two individual translations of this time stand out in particular: *The New Testament in Modern English,* by J. B. Phillips; and *The Living Bible,* by Kenneth Taylor.

    b. Phillips' Translation (1958). In 1941 J. B. Phillips, a vicar in the Church of England, was in charge of a large group of young people in southeast London. Night after night enemy bombers swept in over the city in the terrible blitzes of that memorable winter of World War II.

Phillips tried reading the Bible to his parishioners to give them some assurance. He discovered they had difficulty grasping the language of the King James Version. So he began making a fresh, easy-to-read rendering of Paul's letters for their benefit. Immediately the Bible came alive.

The first letter translated was Colossians. C. S. Lewis, the famous teacher of literature at both Oxford and Cambridge universities, saw a copy. He wrote to Phillips, "It is like seeing an old picture which has been cleaned." He encouraged him to keep up his work. The result was the publication of *Letters to Young Churches* in 1948.

J. B. Phillips had a genius for saying the right thing in the right way. We can cite only a few examples. His translation of 1 Corinthians 8:2 reads, "For whatever a man may know, he still has a lot to learn." Here is another: "I am no shadowboxer; I really fight!" (1 Corinthians 9:26). Quoted frequently is this: "Don't let the world around you squeeze you into its own mould" (Romans 12:2).

These samples underscore an obvious truth: Every good translation, especially a freer one, constitutes a form of commentary. The more of these modern-speech translations one reads, the more fresh insights from Scripture are received. Reading from a different translation of the New Testament each year in private devotions increases one's knowledge of the Word of God. At the rate of a chapter a day, a person can read through the New Testament in less than a year.

c. *The Living Bible (1971)*. An even more popular paraphrase also appeared in several installments. As in the case of Phillips' translation, the volume of the New Testament letters, *Living Letters*, appeared first (1962). It was an immediate success. Teenagers especially enjoyed reading it. It made difficult passages in Paul's letters live for all ages. *Living Gospels* and *Living Prophecies* completed the New Testament. The entire *Living Bible* was published in 1971 and quickly became one of the best selling books in America. According to its publisher, over forty million copies were sold during the last quarter of the twentieth century.

At first Tyndale House of Wheaton, Illinois, published these volumes anonymously. Eventually it was revealed that Kenneth Taylor was the main translator. Taylor was not a Bible scholar, but he was gifted with words. His primary inspiration for his paraphrase had been to make the Bible understandable to his children during family devotions.

This new version is openly described on the title page as a paraphrase. It is a free rendering in many places and often interpretive. This is both an asset and a liability. If the interpretation is correct, it adds to the reader's understanding. However, if the interpretation is incorrect, the reader is led astray. For this reason many Evangelicals prefer translations closer to the Greek text.

d. *The Message (2002)*. Toward the end of the twentieth century a new paraphrase of the Bible began growing in popularity. It also came in installments, with the New Testament appearing in 1993 and various portions of the Old Testament coming out until completed in 2002.

The goal of its translator, Eugene Peterson, was "not to render a word-for-word conversion of Greek into English, but rather to convert the tone, the rhythm, the events, the ideas, into the way we actually think and speak."[3] Peterson, a prominent pastoral theologian, was a biblical languages scholar before serving as a pastor for many years. His capacity for putting biblical ideas into striking phrases made this version quite popular with the younger generation. One example of his lively style is found in his rendering of Ephesians 6:12—"This is no afternoon athletic contest that we'll walk away from and forget about in a couple of hours. This is for keeps, a life-or-death fight to the finish against the Devil and all his angels."

Committee Translations

Though the King James Version has been rightly recognized as "the noblest monument of English prose," it became increasingly clear it did not meet the need of modern readers. The meanings of many of its English words had changed since 1611 (the period of Shakespeare). The most serious problem centered on words that had come to mean exactly the opposite of what they did in 1611. Over eight hundred words and phrases in the King James Version are not used in the same sense today. Of these, about two hundred mean something radically different. *The Bible Word Book*, by Ronald Bridges and Luther Weigle,[4] gives careful discussion of 827 such terms, arranged in alphabetical order.

A further problem is that the King James Version was translated from inferior Greek texts. We have already told the story of Tischendorf's discovery of the Sinaitic manuscript of the Greek Bible in 1859. About the same time, he publicized the only other known Greek manuscript, the Vaticanus, from the fourth century. Kept in the Vatican Library at Rome, Tischendorf gained access to it and revealed the nature of its contents. Today it is considered the most valuable single manuscript of the Greek New Testament. The fifth-century manuscript Alexandrinus reached England in 1627, a few years too late to be used by the King James translators.

Unfortunately, these translators used the Greek text of Erasmus. He had six Greek manuscripts in all—two of the Gospels, two of Paul's epistles, one for Acts and the General Epistles, and one for Revelation. In the Revelation manuscript the final verses were missing. Undaunted, Erasmus translated these verses from Latin. None of his manuscripts were earlier than the tenth century. In other words, the King James Version of the New Testament is based on a late medieval Greek text.

Today we have over 5,000 Greek manuscripts in whole or part of the New Testament. These reach back to the ninth, eighth, seventh, sixth, fifth, and fourth centuries. In the case of the papyri, they go back to the beginning of the second century (about A.D. 125).

a. Revised Version (1885). On the basis of these older manuscripts, B. F. Westcott and F. J. A. Hort worked hard to construct a better Greek text. Though they did not have the papyri, they were able to construct a much more reliable text in the opinion of most scholars. With the development of this better Greek text, scholars increasingly realized the need for a new revision of the Bible in English.

At the Convocation of Canterbury in 1870 the decision was made to revise the King James Version. Old and New Testament companies were appointed. Altogether sixty-five British scholars participated in this project. Included were not only members of the Church of England, Church of Scotland, and Church of Ireland but also Baptists, Methodists, Congregationalists, and Presbyterians. The New Testament was published on May 17, 1881, and a special copy presented to Queen Victoria. Within a few days two million copies of the *Revised New Testament* had been sold. About three million copies were sold the first year. The entire *Revised Bible* appeared in 1885.

The New Testament company had met in the Jerusalem Chamber of Westminster Abbey. Prominent in this group were Westcott and Hort. Their *New Testament in the Original Greek* did not appear until a few days later in 1881, but they made advance sheets available to the revisers as they worked. So the new version was based on a sound Greek text.

b. American Standard Version (1901). The British invited American cooperation in the revision project. An American Committee of Revisers was set up with Philip Schaff as chairman. Some American suggestions were adopted, while others were set aside. The American revisers wanted more drastic changes than did their British colleagues. For example, they wanted "Holy Ghost" changed to "Holy Spirit," since ghost had come to mean the spirit of a dead person. They also proposed the elimination of other out-of-date words and phrases.

It was finally decided to produce a separate edition in the United States. Its official name was "The American Standard Edition of the Revised Version," but it is more commonly known as the *American Standard Version* (ASV). It appeared August 26, 1901.

The English and American editions shared a common fault. Both Spurgeon and Schaff are credited with having summed it up this way: "It is strong in Greek, weak in English." This is because they both sought to stay very literal in translating the Hebrew and Greek, often creating awkward, though accurate, sentences. The *Revised Version* was not suitable for reading in public. It was good for study but not for worship. As a result, it did not gain wide popularity. However, the *American Standard Version* was more widely accepted in the United States than the *Revised Version* was in Britain. The latter was rarely read in British churches.

c. *Revised Standard Version (1952).* The *American Standard Version* (1901) was not really a twentieth-century translation. It still retained the "-eth" endings on verbs and the use of "thee" and "thou." The language was far different from the English spoken at the time.

In 1937 the International Council of Religious Education voted to authorize a revision of the 1901 version. This revision was to "embody the best results of modern scholarship as to the meaning of the Scriptures, and express this meaning in English diction which is designed for use in public and private worship and preserves those qualities which have given to the King James Version a supreme place in English literature."

Thirty-two scholars worked countless hours, without financial remuneration. The New Testament committee convened a total of one hundred forty-five days, besides all the time spent in making the basic translations before the meetings. The New Testament of the *Revised Standard Version* was published in 1946 and the complete Bible in 1952.

In both years a storm of protest swept across the country. Most of it was due to misinformation or ignorance of facts. Probably ninety-five percent of the critical statements were simply not true. For instance, one allegation widely printed stated the RSV translators had "taken the Blood of Christ out of the New Testament" because they did not believe in the atoning sacrifice of Christ. A frequently printed statement said they "omitted the Blood in many passages in the New Testament." Only one such passage exists, Colossians 1:14, where "through his blood" is left out in the *Revised Standard Version*. The reason the translators omitted it is that it is not in any of the early Greek manuscripts. Some later scribe inserted it here from Ephesians 1:7, where it is a genuine reading in the Greek. The RSV translators were honest in translating what they found in the Greek text.

d. New English Bible (1970). In 1961 the New Testament of the *New English Bible* appeared. Unlike the RSV, it was not a revision but a new translation. This was wise. Revisions are always less than ideal.

The *New English Bible* has a freshness and vigor that is positively refreshing. In many places it makes delightful reading. Inevitably there are passages that will not please some readers. No translation fully avoids this fate, for no translation is perfect. Perhaps criticism may be made that it paraphrases too freely at times and introduces interpretations considered objectionable. Like most translations, it can be used helpfully.

The translating was done by the best scholars of Britain, and so it has a distinctive British flavor. The Oxford and Cambridge University presses published the *New English Bible,* complete with Apocrypha, in 1970.

e. New American Bible (1970). The Catholic Biblical Association of America made an excellent translation of the entire Bible from the original Hebrew, Aramaic, and Greek. The Bishop's Committee of the Confraternity of Christian Doctrine sponsored this translation project. It is the first official Catholic Bible in English made from the original languages. We are grateful for this version intended to encourage American Catholics to read their Bibles.

f. New American Standard Bible (1971). During the 1960s a group of conservative Evangelical scholars undertook a revision of the *American Standard Version* of 1901. The New Testament appeared in 1963. It is an excellent translation, presenting a very literal yet readable text. If one wants to know exactly what the Greek text says, he or she will usually find it here. The Old Testament was published in 1971 by the Lockman Foundation, producers of the well-known *Amplified Bible*. In 1995 an updated edition aimed at increased clarity and readability was published.

g. *Today's English Version (1976)*. At first carrying the appealing title *Good News for Modern Man*, this version has had phenomenal sales. Almost immediately after publication of the New Testament in 1968 it sold ten million copies. The full Bible was published in 1976 as the *Good News Bible: The Bible in Today's English Version*. Widely read around the world, it is a product of the American Bible Society.

Some Evangelical scholars have found weaknesses in some passages. One example is in the translation of Sarx (flesh) as "human nature." Yet even with these faults, we rejoice that many people are reading the New Testament in TEV who would otherwise pass it by. We thank God for this.

h. *New International Version (1978)*. As we have noted, the *New American Standard Bible* is a translation for study purposes as well as devotional reading. Its one weakness, perhaps, is that it follows the policy that every Greek word must be represented in English. This results in frequent repetitions and awkward sentences. In the Gospels, for example, the NASB translates the expression "answered and said." Today we would simply say "answered."

In 1965 a group of about forty Evangelical scholars met by invitation in Chicago. Out of this meeting a committee of fifteen was appointed to plan a new, fresh translation in contemporary English "that would have clarity and literary quality and so prove suitable for public and private reading, teaching, preaching, memorization and liturgical use."[5] The aim of this committee was a thoroughly acceptable version to the Evangelical constituency.

They adopted a dynamic-equivalency method for translation. That is, rather than translating word for word or even phrase for phrase, the translators looked for the expression in English that most naturally communicated the message of the original text. The International Bible Society sponsored the project and holds copyright to the translation. The New Testament was completed in 1973 and the Old Testament in 1978. Another edition with minor revisions came out in 1984.

By the beginning of the twenty-first century, the *New International Version* had become the best selling English version in the world. This is due in part to its readability but also to excellent marketing by its publisher.

Few people have any idea of the immense amount of work involved in making a careful translation of the Bible. The process used for the NIV is a good example of such. The author of this book was one of the original fifteen members of the Committee on Bible Translation. He produced the basic translation of Matthew, Mark, and Luke over a period of three years. Translated passages were sent to the executive secretary, Edwin Palmer. He reviewed them, making many suggestions. The author then spent six days, ten hours a day, working with an Intermediate Editorial Committee on Mark's Gospel, two weeks on Matthew, and three weeks on Luke. The results went through a General Editorial Committee, meeting for several weeks at a later date. The translator was then allowed to react to the General Editorial Committee's suggested changes. Finally the Committee on Bible Translation, which had ultimate responsibility for the translation, voted on each proposed change. This is the way each book of the Bible was handled and is the typical process for most committee translations.

i. New King James Version (1982). Most translators in the twentieth and twenty-first centuries have made use of modern

Greek texts when translating the New Testament. *The Greek New Testament,* published by the United Bible Society, and the *Nestle-Aland Novum Testamentum Graece,* from the Institute for New Testament Textual Research, are the standard texts for scholars. Since the publication of Westcott and Hort's 1881 Greek text, scholars have continued to compare readings of ancient manuscripts as new ones were discovered or reevaluated. Over the years committees have worked to come as close as possible to the original words of the New Testament.

One reaction to this trend was the New King James Version. This version did not use the modern Greek texts to improve the King James Version, though it did note alternate readings in footnotes. Rather, the NKJV sought to follow the same purposes of the original translators of the KJV, that was "to make a good translation better." It updated the language of the KJV but retained its memorable expressions wherever possible. The result was a modernized version of the KJV that made the beauty of its phrases more accessible to readers of the twentieth century. The entire Bible was published in 1982, with a second edition containing minor revisions coming in 1984.

j. Tanakh: A New Translation of the Holy Scriptures According to the Traditional Hebrew Text (1985). The Hebrew text used by most translators in the twentieth and twenty-first centuries was based upon a revered ancient text, the Leningrad Codex, from the tenth century. This text is preserved in *Biblica Hebraic Stuttgartensia* with some modifications. Sometimes this text is unintelligible or seems inappropriate to modern translators. In those cases scholars consult the Greek Septuagint or other ancient versions for a more meaningful translation.

In *Tanakh: A New Translation of the Holy Scriptures* Jewish scholars offered a direct translation of the Leningrad Codex as it stands. They made sense of difficult Hebrew words and phrases rather than accept readings from other ancient versions. The Jewish Publication Society, an organization dedicated to making religious materials available to English-speaking Jews, sponsored this project. *The Torah*, the first five books of the Bible, was first published in 1962. Other sections came out in succeeding years until the entire Hebrew Scriptures, the Christian Old Testament, appeared in 1985. Another edition with minor revisions came out in 1999. It is sometimes called the "New JPS Version."

k. New Century Version (1991). The continual desire to make the Bible meaningful for all people produced the *New Century Version*. A first edition of this translation appeared in 1978 as the *English Version for the Deaf*. The goal of its translator, Ervin Bishop, was to make English idioms more understandable to deaf readers. The text continued to be revised in consultation with a committee of scholars and was published as *A New Easy-to-Read Version* (1980), the *International Children's Bible* (1987), and *The Everyday Bible* (1988). Its short sentences and third-grade-level vocabulary make it one of the simplest versions available in English.

l. The Revised English Bible (1989). Oxford and Cambridge University presses undertook a revision of the *New English Bible* in 1989. Scholars who worked on this revision attempted to correct some of the rather free translations for which the NEB was known. In general more conservative in its treatment of the original text than the NEB, it also employed more dignified language and thus served better for liturgical use.

m. New Revised Standard Version (1990). In 1974 the National Council of Churches authorized the revision of the *Revised Standard Version*. Not long before that, in 1971, a second edition of the New Testament portion of the RSV had been issued. The continual discovery and study of ancient manuscripts, particularly the Dead Sea Scrolls, along with advances in understanding the ancient languages, prompted this revision.

Some of the most prestigious biblical scholars of the time made up the committee on translation. The goal was to bring the language of the text up to date with current English usage. Their primary maxim regarding style was "as literal as possible, as free as necessary." Thus, the new revision continued in the same vein as the RSV, being a literal though readable translation.

Of particular interest to this group was the desire to eliminate any gender bias found within the text. Since biblical cultures were primarily male-dominated, references to women are often made with masculine terms. Hebrew has no neuter gender, so it regularly refers to groups of people with masculine terms, even if they include women. The New Testament does the same, though Greek has neuter nouns and pronouns. Sensitivity to gender inclusiveness grew during the later part of the twentieth century. So the translators of the NRSV worked to make the Bible as friendly toward women as toward men. For example, when Paul addresses members of the churches as "brothers" *adelphoi*, the NRSV regularly translates "brothers and sisters." A footnote, however, indicates that the Greek reads simply "brothers."

The NRSV has received wide acceptance among the scholarly community and mainline seminaries and churches. It is often the text of choice for scholarly writing and conferences. Publication of the text in *The New Interpreter's Study Bible, The New Oxford Annotated Bible,* and *The Harper-Collins Study Bible* increased its esteem and usage. Both USA and Canadian Catholic bishops approved the use of a Catholic edition of the NRSV for their members in 1991.

n. New Living Translation (1996). In 1989 Tyndale House brought together ninety leading Evangelical scholars for the purpose of revising the popular *The Living Bible.* Initially the group intended to correct some of the glaring errors and misleading interpretations in that translation. It was finally decided, though, to develop a completely new translation reflecting the spirit of *The Living Bible.*

With the number of people involved and the international scope of the translation committee, this became the most expensive translation project to date. The result was a reader-friendly text easily understood by children and adults alike. It preserved some of the memorable wording of *The Living Bible* but tended to be more faithful to the original languages. It also removed some of the theological biases put forth in *The Living Bible* that were not necessarily in the biblical text.

o. English Standard Version (2001). Highly respected Evangelical pastoral theologian J. I. Packer led a team of over one hundred international Evangelicals in developing the *English Standard Version.* Translators submitted their work to various committees of scholars as well as pastors and leaders of Christian organizations. This helped to ensure accuracy as well as meaningful expression.

The design of this translation was to develop a literal translation using good literary English. The translators endeavored to be "transparent to the original text," which meant they wanted readers to see as much as possible the original structures and meanings in the biblical text. They also relied upon the traditional phrases that have been a part of English translations since the KJV of 1611 and before. Though sensitive to gender issues, this translation did not permit modern English usage to obscure the original expressions of the ancient biblical cultures. For example, "people" is used instead of "men" where both men and women are signified. But the expression "sons of God" is retained in a passage like Romans 8:14 because of its specific reference to inheritance laws of that time.

The ESV broke the trend among most modern translations that leaned toward the thought-for-thought dynamic equivalency approach like the NIV. Even the NKJV and the NRSV, which aimed at being literal, leaned toward the dynamic equivalency method. The value of a more strictly literal approach like that of the ESV has been strongly defended.[6] It is clearly truer to the text and thus less misleading for the reader.

p. Holman Christian Standard Bible (2003). A team of ninety international Bible scholars committed to biblical inerrancy produced the *Holman Christian Standard Bible*. Holman Bible Publishers, the oldest publisher of Bibles in North America, sponsored this project. The philosophy behind this translation is called "optimal equivalency." This approach attempted to strike a balance between "dynamic equivalency" (though-for-thought) and "formal equivalency" (word-for-word) translations in order to avoid the dangers inherent in either one. The danger of the first is that it can become overly interpretive, while the danger of the latter is that it can be too mechanical.

The HCSB contains numerous footnotes that provide the reader with additional information. Sometimes they give a literal translation. Other times they identify alternative English translations or alternative readings from ancient versions.

q. Today's New International Version (2005). Amid considerable controversy, the International Bible Society published a revision of the popular New International Version at the turn of the century. Primary opposition came from conservative Evangelicals who objected to the use of "inclusive language" in the revision. Though such language was used only in reference to people and not God, many major Evangelical leaders protested.

The revision began in 1995 with the publication in England of the New Testament as the *New International Version Inclusive Language Edition*. This received such strong negative reaction that the Bible society reconsidered publishing the text in America. Nevertheless, with the support of a number of leading Evangelical scholars, they proceeded with publication of the New Testament in 2002 and the full Bible in 2005.

Similar to the NRSV, the TNIV attempted to make the Bible friendlier for women readers. It translated "brothers and sisters" instead of "brothers" for *adelphoi* in Paul's letters. In Genesis 1:27 we find that God created "human beings" rather than "man."

Unfortunately, the controversy over gender-sensitive language obscured some of the advances made in this revision. In many places the TNIV corrected some of the NIV's free renderings and became more literal. Recent archaeological and linguistic studies improved a number of other readings as well.

The production of English translations will not likely come to an end soon. Neither will the controversies related them. No translation is perfect. No understanding of Scripture is complete. No language is static. Therefore people will continue trying to improve on our English translations. In each case the hope is that the power of God's Word will be allowed to have its full impact on the minds and hearts of those who read it. "For the word of God is living and active. Sharper than any double-edged sword, it penetrates even to dividing soul and spirit, joints and marrow; it judges the thoughts and attitudes of the heart" (Hebrews 4:12).

Questions

1. What is the significance of John Wesley's translation of the New Testament?

2. What is the main value of a paraphrase like *The Living Bible* or *The Message*?

3. What were the main reasons for revising the King James Version?

4. Compare the *English Standard Version* with the *New International Version,* as far as their objectives and methods are concerned.

5. What makes the *New Revised Standard Version* stand out among the modern translations?

6. Which versions might be most enjoyable just for reading through the text? Which would be better for careful study of particular words and phrases?

Epilogue

Perhaps the author may be allowed to give a word of personal testimony. On Nov. 3, 1922, I accepted Jesus Christ as my Savior and Lord at the close of a Bible study class in a Friends academy. For years I had prayed regularly in family worship and attended church faithfully. My outward life was above reproach. On that day, however, the Holy Spirit through the Word convicted me of the fact that I was a sinner in God's sight.

One of the first fruits of my conversion was a new love for God's Word. For nearly seventy years the Bible has been my daily Companion, giving continual guidance and strength.

There have been three stages in my study of the Bible. The first was a thorough acquaintance with the King James Version in my daily devotions and study of the English Bible for two years in a Bible school.

The second stage was the study of the Greek and Hebrew originals in college, seminary, and university. This was followed by nearly fifty years of teaching the Greek and English New Testament in college and seminary. In addition, I have written about a dozen commentaries on books of the New Testament, all based on a careful study of the Greek text. In the last few years my main concentration has been on translating the New Testament.

Meanwhile, a third stage took place. I discovered a richness of meaning found in the many translations appearing in this century. No single translation in print gives the best rendering of every verse. For various passages in the New Testament one may find clearer and richer rendering in Weymouth, Goodspeed,

Berkeley, Beck, NASB, or the NIV. Paul says, "That ye . . . may be able to comprehend with all saints what is the breadth, and length, and depth, and height" (Ephesians 3:17-18, KJV). Different translators give varying insights into the meaning of particular passages. The student of the Bible will go deeper, higher, wider, and farther in an understanding of the Word by using different translations—though using the NIV in the pulpit.

One word more. This deeper and broader range of Bible study has not robbed me of my early love for the Word of God. Rather, it has deepened my devotion to it, increasing my conviction that the Bible is the inspired Word of God.

Though written by many over a period of a millennium and a half, the miracle of the Bible is its single message of divine redemption. From Genesis to Revelation it tells of our sin, that a holy God cannot condone sin. God's love, however, guarantees forgiveness to all who turn to God in repentance and faith. This message comes through today as clearly as it did nearly 2,000 years ago.

Notes

Chapter 1

1. Samuel M. Powell, *Discovering Our Christian Faith: An Introduction to Theology* (Kansas City: Beacon Hill Press of Kansas City, 2008), 95.

2. H. Ray Dunning, *Grace, Faith and Holiness* (Kansas City: Beacon Hill Press of Kansas City, 1988), 65.

3. James Arminius, *Writings*, trans. James Nichols and W. R. Bagnall (Grand Rapids: Baker Book House, 1956), 2:15.

4. Ibid., 16.

5. John Wesley, *Explanatory Notes upon the New Testament* (London: Epworth Press, 1941), 9.

6. Ibid.

7. Ibid., 794.

8. Frank Moore, *Coffee Shop Theology* (Kansas City: Beacon Hill Press of Kansas City, 1998), 61.

9. W. B. Pope, *A Compendium of Christian Theology*, 2nd ed. (New York: Phillips and Hunt, 1881), 174ff.

10. H. Orton Wiley, *Christian Theology* (Kansas City: Nazarene Publishing House, 1940), 1:168.

11. Ibid., 170.

12. J. Kenneth Grider, *A Wesleyan-Holiness Theology* (Kansas City: Beacon Hill Press of Kansas City, 1994), 68-69.

13. John Wesley, *Works* (Kansas City: Beacon Hill Press of Kansas City, n.d.), vol. 3.

Chapter 3

1. R. K. Harrison, *Introduction to the Old Testament* (Grand Rapids: Wm. B. Eerdmans Publishing Co., 1969), 211.

2. Ibid.

3. B. F. Westcott and F. J. A. Hort, *The New Testament in the Original Greek* (New York: Harper and Brothers, 1882), 2:2.

Chapter 4

1. Augustine, *On Christian Doctrine* [PUBLICATION DATA], 2:13.

2. J. R. Branton, "Versions, English," *The Interpreter's Dictionary of the Bible* (New York: Abingdon Press, 1962), 4:761.

3. Quoted in G. W. Lampe, ed., *The Cambridge History of the Bible* (Cambridge, England: University Press, 1969), 2:388.

4. Ibid.

5. Branton, "Versions," *Interpreter's Dictionary of the Bible*, 4:761.

6. Ibid.

7. Ibid.

8. F. F. Bruce, *The English Bible: A History of Translations* (New York: Oxford University Press, 1961), 31.

9. Branton, "Versions," *Interpreter's Dictionary of the Bible*, 4:762.

10. Herbert Gordon May, *Our English Bible in the Making* (Philadelphia: Westminster Press, 1952), 26.

11. Quoted in Bruce, *The English Bible*, 51-52.

12. Ibid., 107.

13. Geddes MacGregor, *The Bible in the Making* (Philadelphia: J. B. Lippincott Co., 1959), 187.

14. *The Literary Impact of the Authorized Version* (Philadelphia: Fortress Press, 1963), 30.

15. Ibid., 33.

Chapter 5

1. Quoted in John McClintock and James Strong, *Cyclopedia of Biblical, Theological and Ecclesiastical Literature* (Grand Rapids: Baker Book House, 1968, reprint), 2:121.

2. Eric N. North, *The Book of a Thousand Tongues* (New York: Harper and Brothers, 1938), 2.

3. Ibid.

4. Ibid.

5. "Continental Versions to c. 1600," *The Cambridge History of the Bible: The West from the Reformation to the Present Day*, ed. S. L. Greenslade (Cambridge, England: University Press, 1963), 3:103.

6. R. Kilgour, *The Bible Throughout the World* (London: World Dominion Press, 1939), 107.

7. Quoted in McClintock and Strong, *Cyclopedia*, 6:655.

8. Ibid., 33-34.

9. Ibid., 35.

10. Ibid., 61.

11. Ibid., 188.

Chapter 6

1. "English Versions Since 1611," *Cambridge History of the Bible: The West from the Reformation to the Present Day*, S. L. Greenslade, ed. (Cambridge, England: University Press, 1963), 3:361.

2. Ibid., 363.

3. Eugene H. Peterson, *The Message: New Testament with Psalms and Proverbs* (Colorado Springs: NavPress, 1995), 9.

4. Ronald Bridges and Luther Weigle, *The Bible Word Book* (New York: Thomas Nelson and Sons, 1960).

5. "Preface," *The Holy Bible: New International Version* (Nashville: Holman Bible Publishers, 1986).

6. Leland Ryken, *The Word of God in English* (Wheaton, Ill.: Crossway Books, 2002).

Glossary

Apocrypha: books in the Catholic and Orthodox Old Testament that are not in most Protestant Bibles today

Canon: list of books of the Bible officially accepted by the Church to guide belief and practice

Codex: a bound book, in contrast to a roll or scroll

Dead Sea scrolls: manuscripts, mostly biblical, discovered in caves near the Dead Sea

Diaspora: the dispersion or scattering of the Jews beginning about 300 B.C.

Dynamic equivalency: thought-for-thought translation method

Formal equivalency: literal or word-for-word translation method

Inquisition: a Roman Catholic tribunal that suppressed heresy

Manuscript: a handwritten copy of a book

Masoretic Text: Hebrew text of the Old Testament edited by Jewish scribes of the Middle Ages

Minuscules: cursive-style Greek manuscripts of the New Testament written in the ninth to fifteenth centuries

Papyrus: ancient "paper" used as writing material at the time of Christ: —first five books of the Bible

Peshitta: Syriac translation of the Bible

Proselyte: convert to Judaism (or any other religion)

Septuagint: Greek translation of the Old Testament made about 250 to 150 B.C.

Targums: Aramaic paraphrases of the Old Testament

Version: a translation of the Old or New Testament

Vulgate: Latin translation of the Bible made in the fourth century

Uncials: block-style Greek manuscripts of the New Testament written in the third to eleventh centuries

About the Authors

RALPH EARLE served as professor emeritus of New Testament at Nazarene Theological Seminary in Kansas City, where he first began teaching in 1945. While holding pastorates in Woonsocket, Rhode Island, and Everett, Massachusetts, from 1933 to 1945, he was professor of biblical literature at Eastern Nazarene College. He served on the Committee on Bible Translation, which is the governing body for the New International Version of the Bible. Earle earned degrees from Eastern Nazarene College, Boston University, and Gordon Divinity School. He also took postdoctoral courses at Harvard and Edinburgh universities.

JIM EDLIN is professor of biblical literature and languages and the Dean of the School of Religion and Philosophy at MidAmerica Nazarene University. He earned an Mdiv from Nazarene Theological Seminary and a ThM and PhD in Old Testament studies from Southern Baptist Theological Seminary. His previous publications include *NBBC, Daniel* and *Discovering the Old Testament* (Beacon Hill Press). He is a frequent contributor to *Adult Faith Connections* and *Illustrated Bible Life* (WordAction).

STUDY THE STORY AND FAITH OF THE BIBLE

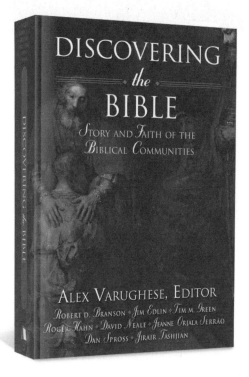

This valuable text is a complete survey of the Bible. With wisdom and scholarly understanding, it examines the Bible's amazing message and story of faith in a way that will captivate readers and impel them to learn more. Its thorough, biblical scholarship; eye-catching format; and easy-to-understand writing style make this textbook a must-have for every Christian's library.

Discovering the Bible
Story and Faith of the Biblical Communities
Alex Varughese, Editor
ISBN: 978-0-8341-2247-5

Also Available:
Discovering the Old Testament
ISBN: 978-0-8341-1994-9

Discovering the New Testament
ISBN: 978-0-8341-2093-8

BEACON HILL PRESS
OF KANSAS CITY

Available online and wherever books are sold.